RESUMES  FOR
ARCHITECTURE AND
RELATED CAREERS

VGM Professional Resumes Series

SECOND EDITION

RESUMES FOR

ARCHITECTURE AND RELATED CAREERS

With Sample Cover Letters

The Editors of VGM Career Books

McGraw·Hill

New York   Chicago   San Francisco   Lisbon   London   Madrid   Mexico City
Milan   New Delhi   San Juan   Seoul   Singapore   Sydney   Toronto

Library of Congress Cataloging-in-Publication Data

Resumes for architecture and related careers / the editors of VGM Career
Books.—2nd ed.
p.   cm. — (VGM professional resumes series)
ISBN 0-07-141161-5 (alk. paper)
1. Architects—Employment—United States.   2. City planners—Employment—
United States.   3. Landscape architects—Employment—United States.
4. Resumes (Employment)—United States.   I. VGM Career Books (Firm)
II. Series.

NA1995.R47   2004
808'.06672—dc22   2003025818

1 2 3 4 5 6 7 8 9 0   QPD/QPD   3 2 1 0 9 8 7 6 5 4

ISBN 0-07-141161-5

McGraw-Hill books are available at special quantity discounts to use as premiums and
sales promotions, or for use in corporate training programs. For more information, please
write to the Director of Special Sales, Professional Publishing, McGraw-Hill, Two Penn
Plaza, New York, NY 10121-2298. Or contact your local bookstore.

This book is printed on acid-free paper.

Contents

Introduction

Your resume is a piece of paper (or an electronic document) that serves to introduce you to the people who will eventually hire you. To write a thoughtful resume, you must thoroughly assess your personality, your accomplishments, and the skills you have acquired. The act of composing and submitting a resume also requires you to carefully consider the company or individual that might hire you. What are they looking for, and how can you meet their needs? This book shows you how to organize your personal information and experience into a concise and well-written resume so that your qualifications and potential as an employee will be understood easily and quickly by a complete stranger.

Writing the resume is just one step in what can be a daunting job-search process, but it is an important element in the chain of events that will lead you to your new position. While you are probably a talented, bright, and charming person, your resume may not reflect these qualities. A poorly written resume can get you nowhere; a well-written resume can land you an interview and potentially a job. A good resume can even lead the interviewer to ask you questions that will allow you to talk about your strengths and highlight the skills you can bring to a prospective employer. Even a person with very little experience can find a good job if he or she is assisted by a thoughtful and polished resume.

Lengthy, typewritten resumes are a thing of the past. Today, employers do not have the time or the patience for verbose documents; they look for tightly composed, straightforward, action-based resumes. Although a one-page resume is the norm, a two-page resume may be warranted if you have had extensive job experience or have changed careers and truly need the space to properly position yourself. If, after careful editing, you still need more than one page to present yourself, it's acceptable to use a second page. A crowded resume that's hard to read would be the worst of your choices.

Distilling your work experience, education, and interests into such a small space requires preparation and thought. This book takes you step-by-step through the process of crafting an effective resume that will stand out in today's competitive marketplace. It serves as a workbook and a place to write down your experiences, while also including the techniques you'll need to pull all the necessary elements together. In the following pages, you'll find many examples of resumes that are specific to your area of interest. Study them for inspiration and find what appeals to you. There are a variety of ways to organize and present your information; inside, you'll find several that will be suitable to your needs. Good luck landing the job of your dreams!

The Elements of an Effective Resume

An effective resume is composed of information that employers are most interested in knowing about a prospective job applicant. This information is conveyed by a few essential elements. The following is a list of elements that are found in most resumes—some essential, some optional. Later in this chapter, we will further examine the role of each of these elements in the makeup of your resume.

- Heading

- Objective and/or Keyword Section

- Work Experience

- Education

- Honors

- Activities

- Certificates and Licenses

- Publications

- Professional Memberships

- Special Skills

- Personal Information

- References

The first step in preparing your resume is to gather information about yourself and your past accomplishments. Later you will refine this information, rewrite it using effective language, and organize it into an attractive layout. But first, let's take a look at each of these important elements individually so you can judge their appropriateness for your resume.

Heading

Although the heading may seem to be the simplest section of your resume, be careful not to take it lightly. It is the first section your prospective employer will see, and it contains the information she or he will need to contact you. At the very least, the heading must contain your name, your home address, and, of course, a phone number where you can be reached easily.

In today's high-tech world, many of us have multiple ways that we can be contacted. You may list your E-mail address if you are reasonably sure the employer makes use of this form of communication. Keep in mind, however, that others may have access to your E-mail messages if you send them from an account provided by your current company. If this is a concern, do not list your work E-mail address on your resume. If you are able to take calls at your current place of business, you should include your work number, because most employers will attempt to contact you during typical business hours.

If you have voice mail or a reliable answering machine at home or at work, list its number in the heading and make sure your greeting is professional and clear. Always include at least one phone number in your heading, even if it is a temporary number, where a prospective employer can leave a message.

You might have a dozen different ways to be contacted, but you do not need to list all of them. Confine your numbers or addresses to those that are the easiest for the prospective employer to use and the simplest for you to retrieve.

Objective

When seeking a specific career path, it is important to list a job or career objective on your resume. This statement helps employers know the direction you see yourself taking, so they can determine whether your goals are in line with those of their organization and the position available. Normally, an objective is one to two sentences long. Its contents will vary depending on your career field, goals, and personality. The objective can be specific or general, but it should always be to the point. See the sample resumes in this book for examples.

If you are planning to use this resume online, or you suspect your potential employer is likely to scan your resume, you will want to include a "keyword" in the objective. This allows a prospective employer, searching hundreds of resumes for a specific skill or position objective, to locate the keyword and find your resume. In essence, a keyword is what's "hot" in your particular field at a given time. It's a buzzword, a shorthand way of getting a particular message across at a glance. For example, if you are a lawyer, your objective might state your desire to work in the area of corporate litigation. In this case, someone searching for the keyword "corporate litigation" will pull up your resume and know that you want to plan, research, and present cases at trial on behalf of the corporation. If your objective states that you "desire a challenging position in systems design," the keyword is "systems design," an industry-specific shorthand way of saying that you want to be involved in assessing the need for, acquiring, and implementing high-technology systems. These are keywords and every industry has them, so it's becoming more and more important to include a few in your resume. (You may need to conduct additional research to make sure you know what keywords are most likely to be used in your desired industry, profession, or situation.)

There are many resume and job-search sites online. Like most things in the online world, they vary a great deal in quality. Use your discretion. If you plan to apply for jobs online or advertise your availability this way, you will want to design a scannable resume. This type of resume uses a format that can be easily scanned into a computer and added to a database. Scanning allows a prospective employer to use keywords to quickly review each applicant's experience and skills, and (in the event that there are many candidates for the job) to keep your resume for future reference.

Many people find that it is worthwhile to create two or more versions of their basic resume. You may want an intricately designed resume on high-quality paper to mail or hand out *and* a resume that is designed to be scanned into a computer and saved on a database or an online job site. You can even create a resume in ASCII text to E-mail to prospective employers. For further information, you may wish to refer to the *Guide to Internet Job Searching*, by Frances Roehm and Margaret Dikel, updated and published every other year by VGM Career Books, a division of the McGraw-Hill Companies. This excellent book contains helpful and detailed information about formatting a resume for Internet use. To get you started, in Chapter 3 we have included a list of things to keep in mind when creating electronic resumes.

Although it is usually a good idea to include an objective, in some cases this element is not necessary. The goal of the objective statement is to provide the employer with an idea of where you see yourself going in the field. However, if you are uncertain of the exact nature of the job you seek, including an objective that is too specific could result in your not being considered for a host of perfectly acceptable positions. If you decide not to use an objective heading in your resume, you should definitely incorporate the information that would be conveyed in the objective into your cover letter.

Work Experience

Work experience is arguably the most important element of them all. Unless you are a recent graduate or former homemaker with little or no relevant work experience, your current and former positions will provide the central focus of the resume. You will want this section to be as complete and carefully constructed as possible. By thoroughly examining your work experience, you can get to the heart of your accomplishments and present them in a way that demonstrates and highlights your qualifications.

If you are just entering the workforce, your resume will probably focus on your education, but you should also include information on your work or volunteer experiences. Although you will have less information about work experience than a person who has held multiple positions or is advanced in his or her career, the amount of information is not what is most important in this section. How the information is presented and what it says about you as a worker and a person are what really count.

As you create this section of your resume, remember the need for accuracy. Include all the necessary information about each of your jobs, including your job title, dates of employment, name of your employer, city, state, responsibilities, special projects you handled, and accomplishments. Be sure to list only accomplishments for which you were directly responsible. And don't be alarmed if you haven't participated in or worked on special projects, because this section may not be relevant to certain jobs.

The most common way to list your work experience is in *reverse chronological order*. In other words, start with your most recent job and work your way backward. This way, your prospective employer sees your current (and often most important) position before considering your past employment. Your most recent position, if it's the most important in terms of responsibilities and relevance to the job for which you are applying, should also be the one that includes the most information as compared to your previous positions.

Even if the work itself seems unrelated to your proposed career path, you should list any job or experience that will help sell your talents. If you were promoted or given greater responsibilities or commendations, be sure to mention the fact.

The following worksheet is provided to help you organize your experiences in the working world. It will also serve as an excellent resource to refer to when updating your resume in the future.

WORK EXPERIENCE

Job One:

Job Title _____

Dates _____

Employer _____

City, State _____

Major Duties _____

_____

_____

_____

_____

_____

_____

_____

_____

Special Projects _____

_____

_____

_____

Accomplishments _____

_____

_____

_____

_____

_____

Job Two:

Job Title _____

Dates _____

Employer _____

City, State _____

Major Duties _____

_____

_____

_____

_____

_____

_____

Special Projects _____

_____

_____

_____

Accomplishments _____

_____

_____

_____

_____

_____

_____

_____

Job Three:

Job Title _____

Dates _____

Employer _____

City, State _____

Major Duties _____

_____

_____

_____

_____

_____

_____

_____

Special Projects _____

_____

_____

_____

Accomplishments _____

_____

_____

_____

_____

_____

_____

_____

Job Four:

Job Title _____

Dates _____

Employer _____

City, State _____

Major Duties _____

_____

_____

_____

_____

_____

_____

_____

_____

Special Projects _____

_____

_____

_____

Accomplishments _____

_____

_____

_____

_____

_____

_____

_____

Education

Education is usually the second most important element of a resume. Your educational background is often a deciding factor in an employer's decision to interview you. Highlight your accomplishments in school as much as you did those accomplishments at work. If you are looking for your first professional job, your education or life experience will be your greatest asset because your related work experience will be minimal. In this case, the education section becomes the most important means of selling yourself.

Include in this section all the degrees or certificates you have received; your major or area of concentration; all of the honors you earned; and any relevant activities you participated in, organized, or chaired. Again, list your most recent schooling first. If you have completed graduate-level work, begin with that and work your way back through your undergraduate education. If you have completed college, you generally should not list your high school experience; do so only if you earned special honors, you had a grade point average that was much better than the norm, or this was your highest level of education.

If you have completed a large number of credit hours in a subject that may be relevant to the position you are seeking but did not obtain a degree, you may wish to list the hours or classes you completed. Keep in mind, however, that you may be asked to explain why you did not finish the program. If you are currently in school, list the degree, certificate, or license you expect to obtain and the projected date of completion.

The following worksheet will help you gather the information you need for this section of your resume.

EDUCATION

School One _____

Major or Area of Concentration _____

Degree _____

Dates _____

School Two _____

Major or Area of Concentration _____

Degree _____

Dates _____

Honors

If you include an honors section in your resume, you should highlight any awards, honors, or memberships in honorary societies that you have received. (You may also incorporate this information into your education section.) Often, the honors are academic in nature, but this section also may be used for special achievements in sports, clubs, or other school activities. Always include the name of the organization awarding the honor and the date(s) received. Use the following worksheet to help you gather your information.

HONORS

Honor One _____

Awarding Organization _____

Date(s) _____

Honor Two _____

Awarding Organization _____

Date(s) _____

Honor Three _____

Awarding Organization _____

Date(s) _____

Honor Four _____

Awarding Organization _____

Date(s) _____

Honor Five _____

Awarding Organization _____

Date(s) _____

Activities

Perhaps you have been active in different organizations or clubs; often an employer will look at such involvement as evidence of initiative, dedication, and good social skills. Examples of your ability to take a leading role in a group should be included on a resume, if you can provide them. The activities section of your resume should present neighborhood and community activities, volunteer positions, and so forth. In general, you may want to avoid listing any organization whose name indicates the race, creed, sex, age, marital status, sexual orientation, or nation of origin of its members because this could expose you to discrimination. Use the following worksheet to list the specifics of your activities.

ACTIVITIES

Organization/Activity _____

Accomplishments _____

_____

_____

Organization/Activity _____

Accomplishments _____

_____

_____

Organization/Activity _____

Accomplishments _____

_____

_____

As your work experience grows through the years, your school activities and honors will carry less weight and be emphasized less in your resume. Eventually, you will probably list only your degree and any major honors received. As time goes by, your job performance and the experience you've gained become the most important elements in your resume, which should change to reflect this.

Certificates and Licenses

If your chosen career path requires specialized training, you may already have certificates or licenses. You should list these if the job you are seeking requires them and you, of course, have acquired them. If you have applied for a license but have not yet received it, use the phrase "application pending."

License requirements vary by state. If you have moved or are planning to relocate to another state, check with that state's board or licensing agency for all licensing requirements.

Always make sure that all of the information you list is completely accurate. Locate copies of your certificates and licenses, and check the exact date and name of the accrediting agency. Use the following worksheet to organize the necessary information.

CERTIFICATES AND LICENSES

Name of License _____

Licensing Agency _____

Date Issued _____

Name of License _____

Licensing Agency _____

Date Issued _____

Name of License _____

Licensing Agency _____

Date Issued _____

Publications

Some professions strongly encourage or even require that you publish. If you have written, coauthored, or edited any books, articles, professional papers, or works of a similar nature that pertain to your field, you will definitely want to include this element. Remember to list the date of publication and the publisher's name, and specify whether you were the sole author or a coauthor. Book, magazine, or journal titles are generally italicized, while the titles of articles within a larger publication appear in quotes. (Check with your reference librarian for more about the appropriate way to present this information.) For scientific or research papers, you will need to give the date, place, and audience to whom the paper was presented.

Use the following worksheet to help you gather the necessary information about your publications.

PUBLICATIONS

Title and Type (Note, Article, etc.) _____

Title of Publication (Journal, Book, etc.) _____

Publisher _____

Date Published _____

Title and Type (Note, Article, etc.) _____

Title of Publication (Journal, Book, etc.) _____

Publisher _____

Date Published _____

Title and Type (Note, Article, etc.) _____

Title of Publication (Journal, Book, etc.) _____

Publisher _____

Date Published _____

Professional Memberships

Another potential element in your resume is a section listing professional memberships. Use this section to describe your involvement in professional associations, unions, and similar organizations. It is to your advantage to list any professional memberships that pertain to the job you are seeking. Many employers see your membership as representative of your desire to stay up-to-date and connected in your field. Include the dates of your involvement and whether you took part in any special activities or held any offices within the organization. Use the following worksheet to organize your information.

PROFESSIONAL MEMBERSHIPS

Name of Organization _____

Office(s) Held_____

Activities _____

Dates _____

Name of Organization _____

Office(s) Held_____

Activities _____

Dates _____

Name of Organization _____

Office(s) Held_____

Activities _____

Dates _____

Name of Organization _____

Office(s) Held_____

Activities _____

Dates _____

Special Skills

The special skills section of your resume is the place to mention any special abilities you have that relate to the job you are seeking. You can use this element to present certain talents or experiences that are not necessarily a part of your education or work experience. Common examples include fluency in a foreign language, extensive travel abroad, or knowledge of a particular computer application. "Special skills" can encompass a wide range of talents, and this section can be used creatively. However, for each skill you list, you should be able to describe how it would be a direct asset in the type of work you're seeking because employers may ask just that in an interview. If you can't think of a way to do this, it may be extraneous information.

Personal Information

Some people include personal information on their resumes. This is generally not recommended, but you might wish to include it if you think that something in your personal life, such as a hobby or talent, has some bearing on the position you are seeking. This type of information is often referred to at the beginning of an interview, when it may be used as an icebreaker. Of course, personal information regarding your age, marital status, race, religion, or sexual orientation should never appear on your resume as personal information. It should be given only in the context of memberships and activities, and only when doing so would not expose you to discrimination.

References

References are not usually given on the resume itself, but a prospective employer needs to know that you have references who may be contacted if necessary. All you need to include is a single sentence at the end of the resume: "References are available upon request," or even simply, "References available." Have a reference list ready—your interviewer may ask to see it! Contact each person on the list ahead of time to see whether it is all right for you to use him or her as a reference. This way, the person has a chance to think about what to say *before* the call occurs. This helps ensure that you will obtain the best reference possible.

Chapter 2

Writing Your Resume

Now that you have gathered the information for each section of your resume, it's time to write it out in a way that will get the attention of the reviewer—hopefully, your future employer! The language you use in your resume will affect its success, so you must be careful and conscientious. Translate the facts you have gathered into the active, precise language of resume writing. You will be aiming for a resume that keeps the reader's interest and highlights your accomplishments in a concise and effective way.

Resume writing is unlike any other form of writing. Although your seventh-grade composition teacher would not approve, the rules of punctuation and sentence building are often completely ignored. Instead, you should try for a functional, direct writing style that focuses on the use of verbs and other words that imply action on your part. Writing with action words and strong verbs characterizes you to potential employers as an energetic, active person, someone who completes tasks and achieves results from his or her work. Resumes that do not make use of action words can sound passive and stale. These resumes are not effective and do not get the attention of any employer, no matter how qualified the applicant. Choose words that display your strengths and demonstrate your initiative. The following list of commonly used verbs will help you create a strong resume:

administered	assembled
advised	assumed responsibility
analyzed	billed
arranged	built

carried out	inspected
channeled	interviewed
collected	introduced
communicated	invented
compiled	maintained
completed	managed
conducted	met with
contacted	motivated
contracted	negotiated
coordinated	operated
counseled	orchestrated
created	ordered
cut	organized
designed	oversaw
determined	performed
developed	planned
directed	prepared
dispatched	presented
distributed	produced
documented	programmed
edited	published
established	purchased
expanded	recommended
functioned as	recorded
gathered	reduced
handled	referred
hired	represented
implemented	researched
improved	reviewed

saved	supervised
screened	taught
served as	tested
served on	trained
sold	typed
suggested	wrote

Let's look at two examples that differ only in their writing style. The first resume section is ineffective because it does not use action words to accent the applicant's work experiences.

WORK EXPERIENCE
Regional Sales Manager

Manager of sales representatives from seven states. Manager of twelve food chain accounts in the East. In charge of the sales force's planned selling toward specific goals. Supervisor and trainer of new sales representatives. Consulting for customers in the areas of inventory management and quality control.

Special Projects: Coordinator and sponsor of annual food-industry sales seminar.

Accomplishments: Monthly regional volume went up 25 percent during my tenure while, at the same time, a proper sales/cost ratio was maintained. Customer-company relations were improved.

In the following paragraph, we have rewritten the same section using action words. Notice how the tone has changed. It now sounds stronger and more active. This person accomplished goals and really *did* things.

WORK EXPERIENCE
Regional Sales Manager

Managed sales representatives from seven states. Oversaw twelve food chain accounts in the eastern United States. Directed the sales force in planned selling toward specific goals. Supervised and trained new sales representatives. Counseled customers in the areas of inventory management and quality control. Coordinated and sponsored the annual Food Industry Seminar. Increased monthly regional volume by 25 percent and helped to improve customer–company relations during my tenure.

One helpful way to construct the work experience section is to make use of your actual job descriptions—the written duties and expectations your employers had for a person in your current or former position. Job descriptions are rarely written in proper resume language, so you will have to rework them, but they do include much of the information necessary to create this section of your resume. If you have access to job descriptions for your former positions, you can use the details to construct an action-oriented paragraph. Often, your human resources department can provide a job description for your current position.

The following is an example of a typical human resources job description, followed by a rewritten version of the same description employing action words and specific details about the job. Again, pay attention to the style of writing instead of the content, as the details of your own experience will be unique.

WORK EXPERIENCE
Public Administrator I

Responsibilities: Coordinate and direct public services to meet the needs of the nation, state, or community. Analyze problems; work with special committees and public agencies; recommend solutions to governing bodies.

Aptitudes and Skills: Ability to relate to and communicate with people; solve complex problems through analysis; plan, organize, and implement policies and programs. Knowledge of political systems, financial management, personnel administration, program evaluation, and organizational theory.

WORK EXPERIENCE
Public Administrator I

Wrote pamphlets and conducted discussion groups to inform citizens of legislative processes and consumer issues. Organized and supervised 25 interviewers. Trained interviewers in effective communication skills.

After you have written out your resume, you are ready to begin the next important step: assembly and layout.

Chapter 3

Assembly and Layout

At this point, you've gathered all the necessary information for your resume and rewritten it in language that will impress your potential employers. Your next step is to assemble the sections in a logical order and lay them out on the page neatly and attractively to achieve the desired effect: getting the interview.

Assembly

The order of the elements in a resume makes a difference in its overall effect. Clearly, you would not want to bury your name and address somewhere in the middle of the resume. Nor would you want to lead with a less important section, such as special skills. Put the elements in an order that stresses your most important accomplishments and the things that will be most appealing to your potential employer. For example, if you are new to the workforce, you will want the reviewer to read about your education and life skills before any part-time jobs you may have held for short durations. On the other hand, if you have been gainfully employed for several years and currently hold an important position in your company, you should list your work accomplishments ahead of your educational information, which has become less pertinent with time.

Certain things should always be included in your resume, but others are optional. The following list shows you which are which. You might want to use it as a checklist to be certain that you have included all of the necessary information.

Essential	**Optional**
Name	Cellular Phone Number
Address	Pager Number
Phone Number	E-Mail Address or Website Address
Work Experience	Voice Mail Number
Education	Job Objective
References Phrase	Honors
	Special Skills
	Publications
	Professional Memberships
	Activities
	Certificates and Licenses
	Personal Information
	Graphics
	Photograph

Your choice of optional sections depends on your own background and employment needs. Always use information that will put you in a favorable light—unless it's absolutely essential, avoid anything that will prompt the interviewer to ask questions about your weaknesses or something else that could be unflattering. Make sure your information is accurate and truthful. If your honors are impressive, include them in the resume. If your activities in school demonstrate talents that are necessary for the job you are seeking, allow space for a section on activities. If you are applying for a position that requires ornamental illustration, you may want to include border illustrations or graphics that demonstrate your talents in this area. If you are answering an advertisement for a job that requires certain physical traits, a photo of yourself might be appropriate. A person applying for a job as a computer programmer would *not* include a photo as part of his or her resume. Each resume is unique, just as each person is unique.

Types of Resumes

So far we have focused on the most common type of resume—the *reverse chronological* resume—in which your most recent job is listed first. This is the type of resume usually preferred by those who have to read a large number of resumes, and it is by far the most popular and widely circulated. However, this style of presentation may not be the most effective way to highlight *your* skills and accomplishments.

For example, if you are reentering the workforce after many years or are trying to change career fields, the *functional* resume may work best. This type of resume puts the focus on your achievements instead of the sequence of your work history. In the functional resume, your experience is presented through your general accomplishments and the skills you have developed in your working life.

A functional resume is assembled from the same information you gathered in Chapter 1. The main difference lies in how you organize the information. Essentially, the work experience section is divided in two, with your job duties and accomplishments constituting one section and your employers' names, cities, and states; your positions; and the dates employed making up the other. Place the first section near the top of your resume, just below your job objective (if used), and call it *Accomplishments* or *Achievements*. The second section, containing the bare essentials of your work history, should come after the accomplishments section and can be called *Employment History*, since it is a chronological overview of your former jobs.

The other sections of your resume remain the same. The work experience section is the only one affected in the functional format. By placing the section that focuses on your achievements at the beginning, you draw attention to these achievements. This puts less emphasis on where you worked and when, and more on what you did and what you are capable of doing.

If you are changing careers, the emphasis on skills and achievements is important. The identities of previous employers (who aren't part of your new career field) need to be downplayed. A functional resume can help accomplish this task. If you are reentering the workforce after a long absence, a functional resume is the obvious choice. And if you lack full-time work experience, you will need to draw attention away from this fact and put the focus on your skills and abilities. You may need to highlight your volunteer activities and part-time work. Education may also play a more important role in your resume.

The type of resume that is right for you will depend on your personal circumstances. It may be helpful to create both types and then compare them. Which one presents you in the best light? Examples of both types of resumes are included in this book. Use the sample resumes in Chapter 5 to help you decide on the content, presentation, and look of your own resume.

Resume or Curriculum Vitae?

A curriculum vitae (CV) is a longer, more detailed synopsis of your professional history, which generally runs three or more pages in length. It includes a summary of your educational and academic background as well as teaching and research experience, publications, presentations, awards, honors, affiliations, and other details. Because the purpose of the CV is different from that of the resume, many of the rules we've discussed thus far involving style and length do not apply.

A curriculum vitae is used primarily for admissions applications to graduate or professional schools, independent consulting in a variety of settings, proposals for fellowships or grants, or applications for positions in academia. As with a resume, you may need different versions of a CV for different types of positions. You should only send a CV when one is specifically requested by an employer or institution.

Like a resume, your CV should include your name, contact information, education, skills, and experience. In addition to the basics, a CV includes research and teaching experience, publications, grants and fellowships, professional associations and licenses, awards, and other information relevant to the position for which you are applying. You can follow the advice presented thus far to gather and organize your personal information.

Special Tips for Electronic Resumes

Because there are many details to consider in writing a resume that will be posted or transmitted on the Internet, or one that will be scanned into a computer when it is received, we suggest that you refer to the *Guide to Internet Job Searching*, by Frances Roehm and Margaret Dikel, as previously mentioned. However, here are some brief, general guidelines to follow if you expect your resume to be scanned into a computer.

- Use standard fonts in which none of the letters touch.

- Keep in mind that underlining, italics, and fancy scripts may not scan well.

- Use boldface and capitalization to set off elements. Again, make sure letters don't touch. Leave at least a quarter inch between lines of type.

- Keep information and elements at the left margin. Centering, columns, and even indenting may change when the resume is optically scanned.

- Do not use any lines, boxes, or graphics.

- Place the most important information at the top of the first page. If you use two pages, put "Page 1 of 2" at the bottom of the first page and put your name and "Page 2 of 2" at the top of the second page.

- List each telephone number on its own line in the header.

- Use multiple keywords or synonyms for what you do to make sure your qualifications will be picked up if a prospective employer is searching for them. Use nouns that are keywords for your profession.

- Be descriptive in your titles. For example, don't just use "assistant"; use "legal office assistant."

- Make sure the contrast between print and paper is good. Use a high-quality laser printer and white or very light colored 8½-by-11-inch paper.

- Mail a high-quality laser print or an excellent copy. Do not fold or use staples, as this might interfere with scanning. You may, however, use paper clips.

In addition to creating a resume that works well for scanning, you may want to have a resume that can be E-mailed to reviewers. Because you may not know what word processing application the recipient uses, the best format to use is ASCII text. (ASCII stands for "American Standard Code for Information Exchange.") It allows people with very different software platforms to exchange and understand information. (E-mail operates on this principle.) ASCII is a simple, text-only language, which means you can include only simple text. There can be no use of boldface, italics, or even paragraph indentations.

To create an ASCII resume, just use your normal word processing program; when finished, save it as a "text only" document. You will find this option under the "save" or "save as" command. Here is a list of things to *avoid* when crafting your electronic resume:

- Tabs. Use your space bar. Tabs will not work.

- Any special characters, such as mathematical symbols.

- Word wrap. Use hard returns (the return key) to make line breaks.

- Centering or other formatting. Align everything at the left margin.

- Bold or italic fonts. Everything will be converted to plain text when you save the file as a "text only" document.

Check carefully for any mistakes before you save the document as a text file. Spell-check and proofread it several times; then ask someone with a keen eye to go over it again for you. Remember: the key is to keep it simple. Any attempt to make this resume pretty or decorative may result in a resume that is confusing and hard to read. After you have saved the document, you can cut and paste it into an E-mail or onto a website.

Layout for a Paper Resume

A great deal of care—and much more formatting—is necessary to achieve an attractive layout for your paper resume. There is no single appropriate layout that applies to every resume, but there are a few basic rules to follow in putting your resume on paper:

- Leave a comfortable margin on the sides, top, and bottom of the page (usually one to one and a half inches).

- Use appropriate spacing between the sections (two to three line spaces are usually adequate).

- Be consistent in the *type* of headings you use for different sections of your resume. For example, if you capitalize the heading EMPLOY-MENT HISTORY, don't use initial capitals and underlining for a section of equal importance, such as Education.

- Do not use more than one font in your resume. Stay consistent by choosing a font that is fairly standard and easy to read, and don't change it for different sections. Beware of the tendency to try to make your resume original by choosing fancy type styles; your resume may end up looking unprofessional instead of creative. Unless you are in a very creative and artistic field, you should almost always stick with tried-and-true type styles like Times New Roman and Palatino, which are often used in business writing. In the area of resume styles, conservative is usually the best way to go.

CHRONOLOGICAL RESUME

Kevin Goldberg, AIA
185 Edens Lane
Fort Lauderdale, FL 33340
(305) 555-8986
kevingoldberg@xxx.com

—Client Relations   —Project Management   —Architectural Design

Employment
1998–Present
Self-employed Architectural/Engineering Consultant
Offer comprehensive consulting and subcontracting services. Varied scope and clientele. Recent projects have included: (1) design of Fairview Inn, 12-room luxury hotel with two-acre garden, and (2) design consult on airport control tower at Miami International.

1989–1998
Senior Architect, Ashberry and Royalton
Full range of responsibilities, including contract negotiations, preparation of client proposals, cost estimating, and field observation on large- and small-scale commercial and residential projects.

1985–1989
Engineering Design Consultant, Wexler Industries
Materials and design consultant for architectural design firm specializing in commercial high-rise construction. Position included job bidding, materials selection, and space planning. Created block and test layouts and stacking plans.

Credentials
American Institute of Architects (AIA)
Florida Architectural License #R3042
Bachelor's degree, Architecture, University of Maryland
Master's degree, Structural Engineering, MIT

References Available

FUNCTIONAL RESUME

CHRIS ABSHIRE

127 Main Street   (513) 205-5555 (Cell)
Madison, WI 53726   (513) 555-1234 (Home)
                                                   chrisabshire@xxx.com

Objective

Opportunity for continued professional development and community service providing educational development services to a mid-size nonprofit group

Experience

Evanston Public Library
Director of Educational Development Programs
September 1999 to Present

Design and implement educational programs in the following areas: literacy, computer education, community special interest, fine arts, book clubs, homework assistance, story hours. Implemented fund-raising and grant-writing projects that increased department's budget by 15 percent. Recently awarded $5,000 grant from Literacy Volunteers of America. Designed and conducted Historic Home Tour.

Walker Science Museum
Manager, Children's Discovery Center
January 1992 to September 1999

Supervised and enhanced visitor use of enclosed children's center within museum. Designed and supervised special events.

Education

B.S. Education, Northern Illinois University, 1994

References

Available on Request

- Always try to fit your resume on one page. If you are having trouble with this, you may be trying to say too much. Edit out any repetitive or unnecessary information, and shorten descriptions of earlier jobs where possible. Ask a friend you trust for feedback on what seems unnecessary or unimportant. For example, you may have included too many optional sections. Today, with the prevalence of the personal computer as a tool, there is no excuse for a poorly laid out resume. Experiment with variations until you are pleased with the result.

Remember that a resume is not an autobiography. Too much information will only get in the way. The more compact your resume, the easier it will be to review. If a person who is swamped with resumes looks at yours, catches the main points, and then calls you for an interview to fill in some of the details, your resume has already accomplished its task. A clear and concise resume makes for a happy reader and a good impression.

There are times when, despite extensive editing, the resume simply cannot fit on one page. In this case, the resume should be laid out on two pages in such a way that neither clarity nor appearance is compromised. Each page of a two-page resume should be marked clearly: the first should indicate "Page 1 of 2," and the second should include your name and the page number, for example, "Julia Ramirez—Page 2 of 2." The pages should then be stapled together. You may use a smaller font (in the same font as the body of your resume) for the page numbers. Place them at the bottom of page one and the top of page two. Again, spend the time now to experiment with the layout until you find one that looks good to you.

Always show your final layout to other people and ask them what they like or dislike about it, and what impresses them most when they read your resume. Make sure that their responses are the same as what you want to elicit from your prospective employer. If they aren't the same, you should continue to make changes until the necessary information is emphasized.

Proofreading

After you have finished typing the master copy of your resume and before you have it copied or printed, thoroughly check it for typing and spelling errors. Do not place all your trust in your computer's spell-check function. Use an old editing trick and read the whole resume backward—start at the end and read it right to left and bottom to top. This can help you see the small errors or inconsistencies that are easy to overlook. Take time to do it right because a single error on a document this important can cause the reader to judge your attention to detail in a harsh light.

Have several people look at the finished resume just in case you've missed an error. Don't try to take a shortcut; not having an unbiased set of eyes examine your resume now could mean embarrassment later. Even experienced editors can easily overlook their own errors. Be thorough and conscientious with your proofreading so your first impression is a perfect one.

We have included the following rules of capitalization and punctuation to assist you in the final stage of creating your resume. Remember that resumes often require use of a shorthand style of writing that may include sentences without periods and other stylistic choices that break the standard rules of grammar. Be consistent in each section and throughout the whole resume with your choices.

RULES OF CAPITALIZATION

- Capitalize proper nouns, such as names of schools, colleges, and universities; names of companies; and brand names of products.

- Capitalize major words in the names and titles of books, tests, and articles that appear in the body of your resume.

- Capitalize words in major section headings of your resume.

- Do not capitalize words just because they seem important.

- When in doubt, consult a style manual such as *Words into Type* (Prentice Hall) or *The Chicago Manual of Style* (The University of Chicago Press). Your local library can help you locate these and other reference books. Many computer programs also have grammar help sections.

RULES OF PUNCTUATION

- Use commas to separate words in a series.

- Use a semicolon to separate series of words that already include commas within the series. (For an example, see the first rule of capitalization.)

- Use a semicolon to separate independent clauses that are not joined by a conjunction.

- Use a period to end a sentence.

- Use a colon to show that examples or details follow that will expand or amplify the preceding phrase.

- Avoid the use of dashes.

- Avoid the use of brackets.

- If you use any punctuation in an unusual way in your resume, be consistent in its use.

- Whenever you are uncertain, consult a style manual.

Putting Your Resume in Print

You will need to buy high-quality paper for your printer before you print your finished resume. Regular office paper is not good enough for resumes; the reviewer will probably think it looks flimsy and cheap. Go to an office supply store or copy shop and select a high-quality bond paper that will make a good first impression. Select colors like white, off-white, or possibly a light gray. In some industries, a pastel may be acceptable, but be sure the color and feel of the paper makes a subtle, positive statement about you. Nothing in the choice of paper should be loud or unprofessional.

If your computer printer does not reproduce your resume properly and produces smudged or stuttered type, either ask to borrow a friend's or take your disk (or a clean original) to a printer or copy shop for high-quality copying. If you anticipate needing a large number of copies, taking your resume to a copy shop or a printer is probably the best choice.

Hold a sheet of your unprinted bond paper up to the light. If it has a watermark, you will want to point this out to the person helping you with copies; the printing should be done so that the reader can read the print and see the watermark the right way up. Check each copy for smudges or streaks. This is the time to be a perfectionist—the results of your careful preparation will be well worth it.

The Cover Letter

Once your resume has been assembled, laid out, and printed to your satisfaction, the next and final step before distribution is to write your cover letter. Though there may be instances where you deliver your resume in person, you will usually send it through the mail or online. Resumes sent through the mail always need an accompanying letter that briefly introduces you and your resume. The purpose of the cover letter is to get a potential employer to read your resume, just as the purpose of the resume is to get that same potential employer to call you for an interview.

Like your resume, your cover letter should be clean, neat, and direct. A cover letter usually includes the following information:

1. Your name and address (unless it already appears on your personal letterhead) and your phone number(s); see item 7.

2. The date.

3. The name and address of the person and company to whom you are sending your resume.

4. The salutation ("Dear Mr." or "Dear Ms." followed by the person's last name, or "To Whom It May Concern" if you are answering a blind ad).

5. An opening paragraph explaining why you are writing (for example, in response to an ad, as a follow-up to a previous meeting, at the suggestion of someone you both know) and indicating that you are interested in whatever job is being offered.

6. One or more paragraphs that tell why you want to work for the company and what qualifications and experiences you can bring to the position. This is a good place to mention some detail about

that particular company that makes you want to work for them; this shows that you have done some research before applying.

7. A final paragraph that closes the letter and invites the reviewer to contact you for an interview. This can be a good place to tell the potential employer which method would be best to use when contacting you. Be sure to give the correct phone number and a good time to reach you, if that is important. You may mention here that your references are available upon request.

8. The closing ("Sincerely" or "Yours truly") followed by your signature in a dark ink, with your name typed under it.

Your cover letter should include all of this information and be no longer than one page in length. The language used should be polite, businesslike, and to the point. Don't attempt to tell your life story in the cover letter; a long and cluttered letter will serve only to annoy the reader. Remember that you need to mention only a few of your accomplishments and skills in the cover letter. The rest of your information is available in your resume. If your cover letter is a success, your resume will be read and all pertinent information reviewed by your prospective employer.

Producing the Cover Letter

Cover letters should always be individualized because they are always written to specific individuals and companies. Never use a form letter for your cover letter or copy it as you would a resume. Each cover letter should be unique, and as personal and lively as possible. (Of course, once you have written and rewritten your first cover letter until you are satisfied with it, you can certainly use similar wording in subsequent letters. You may want to save a template on your computer for future reference.) Keep a hard copy of each cover letter so you know exactly what you wrote in each one.

There are sample cover letters in Chapter 6. Use them as models or for ideas of how to assemble and lay out your own cover letters. Remember that every letter is unique and depends on the particular circumstances of the individual writing it and the job for which he or she is applying.

After you have written your cover letter, proofread it as thoroughly as you did your resume. Again, spelling or punctuation errors are a sure sign of carelessness, and you don't want that to be a part of your first impression on a prospective employer. This is no time to trust your spell-check function. Even after going through a spelling and grammar check, your cover letter should be carefully proofread by at least one other person.

Print the cover letter on the same quality bond paper you used for your resume. Remember to sign it, using a good dark-ink pen. Handle the letter and resume carefully to avoid smudging or wrinkling, and mail them together in an appropriately sized envelope. Many stores sell matching envelopes to coordinate with your choice of bond paper.

Keep an accurate record of all resumes you send out and the results of each mailing. This record can be kept on your computer, in a calendar or notebook, or on file cards. Knowing when a resume is likely to have been received will keep you on track as you make follow-up phone calls.

About a week after mailing resumes and cover letters to potential employers, contact them by telephone. Confirm that your resume arrived and ask whether an interview might be possible. Be sure to record the name of the person you spoke to and any other information you gleaned from the conversation. It is wise to treat the person answering the phone with a great deal of respect; sometimes the assistant or receptionist has the ear of the person doing the hiring.

You should make a great impression with the strong, straightforward resume and personalized cover letter you have just created. We wish you every success in securing the career of your dreams!

Sample Resumes

This chapter contains dozens of sample resumes for people pursuing a wide variety of jobs and careers.

There are many different styles of resumes in terms of graphic layout and presentation of information. These samples represent people with varying amounts of education and experience. Use them as models for your own resume. Choose one resume or borrow elements from several different resumes to help you design your own.

Monica Porter, AIA

4311 N. Barrington Road
Chicago, IL 60648
312-555-4949
monicaporter@xxx.com

Goal

Professional opportunity with architectural firm that requires specialized
knowledge in the areas of land development, facilities management, and
architectural design.

Employers

Wright Builders, Chicago Project Architect 1998-Present
Review and develop schematic drawings for commercial and industrial
construction firm. Select and establish building sites. Solicit and review
subcontractor bids. Produce specifications, blueprints, and scale models.

Porter and Stern, AIA, Chicago Project Coordinator 1996-1998
Specified project parameters. Established budgets and schedules. 100
percent of projects completed on time and within budget. Reviewed and
modified all construction documentation: specifications, schematics, etc.

Harrison Design, Inc., New York City, Design Draftsman 1994-1996
Produced computer design sketches, blueprints, layouts, and stacking
diagrams for high-rise commercial projects.

Credentials

B. Arch. University of Illinois, Chicago 1994
Licensed Architect
Professional Draftsman
Computer Literate
Member, American Institute of Architects

References Available

Charlotte Epson

540 Dalton Road
Arlington, Virginia 22202
703-555-6812
charlotteepson@xxx.com

Experienced architectural technologist with expertise in:
- writing and project specifications
- interpreting architectural plans
- creating project proposals
- producing scale models

Work History

Olson Architectural Inc.
Arlington, Virginia
Specifications Writer 2003–Present

Reynolds Design Associates
Atlanta, Georgia
Drafter 2000–2003

Anderson Construction Inc.
Atlanta, Georgia
Drafter 1996–2000

Education

1996 Associate Degree, Drafting—Atlanta College of Design
1992 Graduate—Ryerson Technical High School

References Available

Dan Pendleton

8219 Rogers Road
Anaheim, California 92803
(714) 555-5865
danpendleton@xxx.com

Professional Construction Management

- Extensive experience in all phases of general construction
- Involvement in development and construction of more than 60 structures
- Competent in all phases of general contracting and subcontracting
- Successful in securing financing, zoning, and building permits
- Accurate cost estimating
- Successful job bidding and contract negotiations

Employers

Self-employed
General Contractor 1999-Present

TBS Construction
Construction Supervisor 1996-1999

Madigan Home Builders
Project Coordinator 1991-1996

Sample Projects

Oakton Junior High School
Construction Supervisor

Crestwood Inn
Project Coordinator

Sample Projects (cont.)

Anaheim Health Foods
General Contractor

Tanglewood Housing Development
Project Coordinator

Education

Associate's Degree, Architectural Technology, 1991
California Technical Institute

References

Available Upon Request

Carlotta Hernandez

652 Menard Lane
Boulder, Colorado 80301
(303) 555-5958
carlottahernandez@xxx.com

Background

Hardworking, experienced architectural drafter seeking new professional challenges

Skills

- Ability to develop creative, cost-effective construction plans for residential and commercial building projects
- Experience with AutoCAD and DesignCAD computer programs
- Hands-on construction background
- Complete knowledge of building codes and fire and safety regulations
- Strong work ethic and close attention to detail
- Proven ability to meet deadlines

Employers

1998-Present	S & J Builders, Design Drafter
1996-1998	Trenton Architectural Associates, Design Drafter
1992-1996	Weldon & Sons Construction, Construction Supervisor
1990-1992	Weldon & Sons Construction, Part-time Construction Worker

Education

A.A. Drafting, Colorado Community College

References are available

Landscape Architect

Suzanne Parker

8411 Ainsie Blvd.
Boulder, CO 80304
303-555-6948
suzanneparker@xxx.com

Experience

Parker Design Inc.
Owner of landscape design firm specializing in commercial and multi-unit residential projects. Work in cooperation with architects and interior designers.   1997-Present

Colorado Community College
Lecturer in landscape design. Teach Horticulture I and Basic Landscaping.   1997-Present

Grady Nursery
Assistant manager of nursery. Supervised salespeople, maintained inventory, and scheduled deliveries and landscaping projects.
1994-1997

Awards

Businesswoman of the Year
Denver Businesswomen   2000

Best Landscape Design
Colorado Design Council   1999

Education

University of California at Berkeley
B.S. Landscape Architecture

References available

JOHN HOPEWELL

642 BRADY ROAD • WESTFIELD, NJ 07901
201-555-4900 • CELL: 201-555-7556
JOHNHOPEWELL@XXX.COM

SKILLS

DESIGN

- Conduct preliminary space planning
- Select and specify furniture, equipment, and hardware
- Prepare fixture and architectural design details
- Inspect ceiling condition and determine electrical fixture locations
- Prepare and present preliminary and final design sketches

DOCUMENTATION PREPARATION

- Write specifications for electrical, heating and cooling, air supply, and sprinkler systems
- Write specifications and create design sketches for wall, floor, and ceiling finishes, and all architectural details
- Prepare computer-generated floor layouts
- Coordinate mechanical, electrical, structural, and civil engineering drawings
- Prepare building and site plans
- Create working drawings to secure building permits

SUPERVISION

- Coordinate all phases of architectural projects
- Set schedules
- Supervise interior architectural work
- Review and approve all subcontractor drawings

EMPLOYERS

Westfield Design Group, Westfield, NJ
Project Manager
Oct. 1997-Present

Design Concept Inc., Los Angeles, CA
Design Consultant
Jan. 1995-Sept. 1997

C. J. Partners, Los Angeles, CA
Project Manager
May 1994-Jan. 1995

Culverson Associates, Denver, CO
Project Designer
Oct. 1992-April 1994

EDUCATION

Washington State University
Bachelor of Architecture, 1992

REFERENCES

Available

Erica Martin, AIA

3123 Glenwood Road • Boston, MA 01936
(617) 555-4206 • ericamartin@xxx.com

Background

Twelve years of progressively more responsible experience with nationally known architectural firms. Competent in all areas of design development and project management.

Employment Record

10/98–Present
Woodside Architectural Group, Project Architect

Recent Projects
- Jackson Junior High School
  Project Design and Management
- Hilderbrande School of Music
  Project Design Development
- Culverson Woods Housing Development
  Project Management

11/96–9/98
Hayes Design Limited, Design Drafter

Recent Projects
- Fairfield Resort
  Design Development
- Radley Apartments
  Tenant Improvements

9/93–11/96
    Boston Department of Public Works, Building Inspector

Credentials

Licensed Architect
State of Massachusetts #T6043
Certified Building Inspector
M.S. Arch. University of Maryland
B. Arch. Columbia University

References Available

RICHARD HOPKINS

212 Broad Street
Houston, Texas 94117
713-555-8765
richardhopkins@xxx.com

SKILLS

Community relations
Fund-raising
Cost accounting
Labor mediation
Contract negotiations

EMPLOYERS

2001-Present
Self-employed Business Consultant, Houston, Texas
Assist corporations and entrepreneurs in conducting marketing
studies, designing business proposals, and selecting manufacturing
locations worldwide.

1998-2001
Project Manager, Kincaid Development, Austin, Texas
Managed all aspects of commercial building projects, including site
selection, hiring of architects and builders, budgeting, and contract
negotiations.

1995-1998
Accountant, Martin Mortgage, Dallas, Texas
Responsible for general accounting duties for residential mortgage
firm. Trained loan officers.

EDUCATION

B.A. Accounting, University of Alabama
M.B.A. Southern Methodist University

References Available

Lee Herada

418 Range Road
Buffalo, New York 14225

leeherada@xxx.com
212-555-9867
212-555-7766 (Cell)

Summary

Capable general contractor with wide range of experience in architecture and building trades seeks residential or commercial general or subcontracting assignments.

Work History

2001-Present
Owner, Herada Construction, Inc.
    Self-employed contractor handling project management, field observation, and subcontracting assignments for area architects and builders. Recent projects include design development for Chamber Office Complex and project management on the Carlsburg Public Library expansion project.

1996-2001
Project Manager, Emerson, Inc.
    Produced surveys and studies of land development projects. Responsible for site selection, facilities planning, and floor layout. Prepared models, written proposals, and price quotes for clients. Participated in financial discussions and contract negotiations with architects, attorneys, investors, and contractors.

1994-1996
Design Drafter, Livingston Design Group
    Produced schematics, scale models, and preliminary sketches for architects.

Credentials

M.B.A.
1996 Syracuse University

A.A. Drafting
1992 New York School of Design

Member, American Home Builders Association

References

Charles Berman, Partner
Berman & Brad, AIA
212-555-4899
charlesberman@xxx.com

Renu Sikatt, AIA
Emerson, Inc.
212-555-7000
renusikatt@xxx.com

Martin Pinkman, City Planning Director
Carlsburg, NY
212-555-4958
martinpinkman@xxx.com

LAURA RYERSON, AIA

650 SANDERS ROAD
EAST HAMPTON, NY 11937
(212) 555-4260
(212) 555-5270 - Cell Phone
lauraryerson@xxx.com

EXPERTISE

Project coordination, space planning, facilities management, construction supervision.

EMPLOYERS

7/98-Present, Project Coordinator
EVERLY AND SCOTT, AIA, East Hampton
Create and review construction documents and schematics. Develop project guidelines, establish schedules and budgets. Solicit bids and finalize contracts.

> PROJECTS
> Architectural Designer
> Rosebud Office Complex
> Designed 8,000-square-foot office space.
>
> Architectural Consultant
> University of Phoenix
> College of Business
> Prepared cost analysis and feasibility studies for design team.

6/96-6/98, Project Architect
SANTIAGO AND MENENDEZ, INC., New York City
Coordinated work of subcontractors. Supervised interior construction. Set schedules and budgets. Solicited bids and finalized contracts.

> PROJECTS
> Architectural Designer
> Lovejoy School of Performing Arts
> Reviewed project plan and redesigned studio/rehearsal space. Reduced materials costs by 15 percent.

EMPLOYERS (cont.)

5/94-6/96, Project Coordinator
FINNERTY DESIGN INC., Boston
Reviewed budgets and bids from subcontractors. Analyzed and revised schematic drawings. Prepared and presented client proposals.

PROJECTS
Architectural Designer
Waverly Medical Clinic
Created successful bid and design for 4,000-square-foot medical clinic. Design included on-site medical lab.

4/90-5/94, Design Drafter
FORUM DESIGN, New York City
Prepared construction documents, design sketches, and scale models.

CREDENTIALS

Registered Architect
New York and Massachusetts

Syracuse University
Bachelor of Architecture, 1990

Member, American Institute of Architects

REFERENCES

Available

Barbara Remington

322 Harrison Street
St. Louis, MO 63146
800-555-9866
barabararemington@xxx.com

Background

Owner of successful home inspection service serving real estate professionals and home buyers.

Job History

1997–Present
Owner, Remington Home Inspection, Inc., St. Louis
Own and manage home inspection service employing five full-time staff members. Analyze structures for compliance to building and safety codes. Check all appliances, electrical outlets, walls, ceilings, floors, and foundations. Issue written reports on building status.

1995–1997
Building Inspector, Patterson Home Inspection, Chicago
Inspected residential and commercial properties. Checked structural integrity and heating, cooling, and electrical systems. Inspected roofing and foundations for signs of damage. Prepared reports for superiors and clients.

1992–1995
Building Inspector, City of Chicago
Inspected structures and enforced city fire, safety, and building codes. Issued safety citations and warnings. Conducted follow-up inspections to ensure corrective action was taken.

Credentials

Licensed building inspector, Missouri and Illinois
A.A. Wright College, Business/Building Trades

References

Available

Linda Carsten

221 Chandler Road
Neavitt, MD 21652
410-555-9532
lindacarsten@xxx.com

Abilities
- Knowledge of interior design
- Sales experience
- Customer service skills
- Computer skills
- Strong work ethic

Education
Interior Design, University of Maryland
Degree expected Spring 2004

Job History
Student Assistant
Campus Activities Office
2002-Present
- Provide clerical support to Student Activities Director and assist in publicizing campus events. Create, duplicate, and post flyers. Develop and place ads.

Salesperson
Memory Lane Antiques
Summers 2000 and 2002
- Assisted store manager in providing customer service, arranging merchandise, and restoring antique furniture.

References
Karen Stafford, Owner
Memory Lane Antiques
410-555-4095
karenstafford@xxx.com

Steve King, Instructor
University of Maryland
410-555-6140
steveking@xxx.com

Sean Clark

618 Emerson Street • Atlanta, Georgia 30356

(404) 555-1932 • (404) 555-6655

seanclark@xxx.com

Background

Experienced interior designer specializing in textiles and fine furnishings.

Employers

Limelight Design, Design Consultant, 2001-Present
Assist interior designer in recommending textiles, furnishings, and floor plans for residential decorating projects.

Martex Textiles, Inc., Textile Designer, 1999-2001
Created original fabric designs for textile manufacturer. Specialized in reinterpretations of 18th-century patterns for use in fabrics and wall coverings.

Liberty Home Furnishings, Salesperson, 1996-1999
Assisted customers in selecting furniture, finishes, fabrics, and accessories. Used computer design system to illustrate possible color schemes and floor layouts.

Education

B.A. University of Georgia
Decorative Arts and Design 1998

Rayburn Community College
Courses in drafting and computer science

Memberships

American Society of Interior Designers
Southern Design Council

Awards

Best New Textile Design: "American Rose" pattern
Southern Design Council

Honorable Mention: Fabric Design
Atlanta Showcase Home
American Society of Interior Designers

References

Cathy Walker, Manager
Liberty House Home Furnishings
(404) 555-6968
cathywalker@xxx.com

Martin Lee, Vice President of Design
Martex Textile, Inc.
(404) 555-4958
martinlee@xxx.com

Carol Parker, Designer
Limelight Designs
(404) 555-4940, ext. 399
carolparker@xxx.com

Design portfolio available for review online: www.seanclark.com

CARL ANDERSON

819 Nestle Road • Brooklyn, New York 10036
(212) 555-4857 • carlanderson@xxx.com

Experienced drafter seeking employment with established architectural firm.

WORK HISTORY

2000-Present
Specification Writer
Warner Architectural

- Design building specifications
- Interpret architectural plans
- Supervise construction site

1998-2000
Draftsman
Browne and Sons, AIA

- Interpreted blueprints
- Produced scale models

1995-1998
Construction Supervisor
Keller Construction

- Directed construction crews
- Assured safety and quality control on-site

EDUCATION

A.A. Drafting
1995 Brooklyn Community College

Graduated with Honors
1993 Brooklyn Vocational High School

References Available

Tina Roberts

1810 Jacob Street   Chicago, IL 60648   (312) 555-5968

Professional Abilities
Community Development
Fund-Raising
Grant Writing
Site Selection
Building Inspection

Job History
Tillman Business Consultant   Real Estate Analyst   2001-Present
- Assist businesses considering relocation. Research vacancy rates, mortgage rates, and availability. Assess clients' needs and develop relocation strategies with input from community leaders and business investors. Prepare oral and written client presentations.

Tulsa Public Works Department   Building Inspector   1995-2001
- Inspected structures on behalf of City of Tulsa to ensure compliance with municipal building codes. Submitted recommendations to City Council regarding building permits.

Tulsa Public Works Department   Relocation Counselor   1992-1995
- Counseled residents during housing conversion and advised them of their options. Suggested sources of housing assistance and low-cost loans.

Education
B.A. University of Chicago, Urban Studies and Business Management, 1992

References Available

Paul Knight

107 Jessop Street • San Francisco, CA 94107 • (415) 555-4958

Summary

Experienced landscape architect
Owner, successful landscaping firm
Skilled builder

Employment

Owner
Knight Landscapes 2000-Present
Manage landscaping firm employing six full-time staff members. Offer clients complete landscape design and installation, including selection and placement of plants and construction of arbors, fountains, gazebos, and other exterior structures.

Landscape Architect
Anderson Nursery 1998-2000
Responsible for all aspects of landscape design. Provided clients with complete proposals, including preliminary sketches and cost estimates.

Journeyman Carpenter
Guild Builders 1996-1998
Assisted residential builder specializing in outdoor remodeling projects: solariums, decks, etc. Completed all projects within budget and deadline and to clients' satisfaction.

Education

B.A. Landscape Design
Claremont College

A.A. Carpentry
Lawrence Community College

Memberships

American Home Builders Association
California Council on Landscape Design

References

Personal and professional references available

James Bernard

4611 Ebberts Lane
Ellison Bay, Wisconsin 54210
(414) 555-6978
jamesbernard@xxx.com

Background

Professional accountant with extensive experience serving the real estate and building trades industries. Seeking new opportunities to combine accounting skills with interest in architecture and real estate.

Employment History

Budget Analyst   Barlow Architectural Group   2001-Present
• Responsibilities include productivity studies, inventory control, cost estimating, budgeting, auditing, and quality control.

Project Manager   Corrigan Construction   1999-2001
• Directed all financial aspects of construction projects. Responsibilities included cost estimating and developing client proposals. Hired subcontractors and finalized contracts.

Accountant   Springfield Financial Group   1997-1999
• Entry-level accountant for business/financial consultants specializing in providing financial planning for real estate developers.

Education

B.S. Accounting   University of Wisconsin, Madison 1997

Michael Gifford

(404) 555-0909
1822 S. Jackson Street
Atlanta, Georgia 30356
Michaelgifford@xxx.com

Professional Strengths

- Skilled carpenter with residential and commercial building experience
- Careful analysis of blueprints and schematics
- Adherence to budget and time limits
- On-site supervision of building projects
- Selection and preparation of sites
- Surveying and drafting experience

Work History

Construction Supervisor
    McHale Custom Builders, Atlanta, Georgia
    2001-Present

Independent Contractor
    Boulder, Colorado
    1997-2001

Carpenter
    Parkerson Construction, Denver, Colorado
    1994-1997

Qualifications

Surveying and Drafting Courses
Westwood Community College
Denver, Colorado
    1992-1994

References

Available on Request

Claude Montgomery, AIA

8246 Marquette Road
Chicago, IL 60657
312-555-9656
claudemontgomery@xxx.com

• Background

Work for local architectural firms and community development organizations dedicated to revitalizing inner-city neighborhoods through the creation of affordable housing. Experienced in all phases of residential design and project management.

• Employers

Martin & O'Brien Builders   1999-Present
Project Manager

Direct successful housing construction and rehabilitation projects. Consult with city officials regarding site selection for scattered low-cost housing. Liaison between architects, builders, community leaders, and government officials. Manage staff of four. Supervise and coordinate work of all subcontractors. Responsible for field observation and status reports. Currently working on $5 million expansion/redesign of community centers for Chicago City Housing Authority.

Wakefield Construction   1996-1999
Project Architect

Varied experience in all phases of residential and commercial property design. Established budgets; successfully contained building costs; presented design and budget proposals to clients, investors, and city officials. Secured building and zoning permits. Monitored progress of jobs on-site.

• Credentials

Licensed, State of Illinois
B. Arch. University of Illinois, Chicago 1996

References on Request

Casey Corbett, AIA

8162 Alden Road
Morrisville, VT 05661
802-555-4553
caseycorbett@xxx.com

Goal

Further professional experience in all phases of general contracting and subcontracting.

Assets

Licensed architect
Certified land surveyor
Extensive knowledge of architecture, urban planning, and historic preservation
Effective supervisor
Strong written and oral communication skills
Computer design/drafting skills

Work History

2001-Present
Board Member
New England Architectural Association
- Chair Committee on Historic Preservation, dedicated to identifying and preserving historically and architecturally significant structures throughout New England.

2001-Present
Project Architect
Charles DuMont & Associates
- Direct all phases of residential construction projects. Specialize in redesigning and rehabilitation of 19th-century homes. Complete responsibility for setting project parameters, hiring subcontractors, developing client proposals, and supervising work on-site.

Work History (cont.)

1997-2001
Construction Supervisor
Melton Construction
- Selected and established construction sites. Surveyed and pinned lot lines. Solicited bids from subcontractors and finalized contracts.

1994-1997
Community Development Specialist
Vermont Housing Commission
- Studied statewide housing patterns and created community development proposals for governor's commission. Designed census and survey documents.

Education

B. Arch.	University of Maryland	1994
B.A.	University of Virginia	1992
	Major: Urban Studies	
	Minor: Statistics	

Memberships

American Institute of Architects
New England Architectural Association

References

On Request

Felicia Lowell

4211 Windward Road
Grand Rapids, MI 49505
616-555-8988
felicialowell@xxx.com

Goal

Position as drafter for a mid-size architectural firm
that rewards talent and hard work.

Work History

2002-Present
Drafter, Marilyn Quindlen, AIA, Grand Rapids, MI
• Drafter, AutoCAD designer, and field rep for local
architect specializing in residential design.

1999-2002
Drafter, Perkins Architectural Group, Grandville, MI
• Drafter, surveyor, and design assistant to architects.

1996-1999
Drafter, Sharper Image Design, Inc., Portage, MI
• Drafter, designer, and general assistant to architects
and interior designers.

Education

Drafting Technology
North Park College
Graduated, 1996

References Available

Kim Delaney
Landscape Designer

766 Warren Road • Miami, Florida 33152
Kimdelaney@xxx.com • 305-555-9595 Cell • 305-555-5590 Home

Skills

Landscape Design
Project Management
Creation of Design Sketches and Scale Models
Supervision of Subcontractors
Successful Collaboration with Architects and Interior Designers

Employment History

2000-Present	Owner	Custom Landscapes, Inc.
1999-2000	Landscape Designer	White Oak Nursery
1996-1999	General Manager	Evergreen Lawn Care

Education

1995	B.A. in Landscape Design
	Florida State University

References

Business references, personal references, and portfolio available on request.

Gary Snyder

877 Lindenhurst Lane
Kansas City, MO 64108
(816) 555-5867
garysnyder@xxx.com

• Background

Experienced interior designer seeking new projects and new ways to expand my knowledge of the decorative arts.

• Employers

Midwest Design Limited 1995-Present
Interior Design Specialist
Create personalized color schemes and textile designs for interior design firm. Work as part of a team. Specialize in textiles, window treatments, and lines.

Alcea Textiles Inc. 1993-1995
Assistant Textile Designer
Worked with local artisan creating handcrafted fabrics and silk screens for home fashions. Created special-order upholstered pieces and sub-contracted for local furniture and draperies stores.

Palace Antiques 1989-1993
Co-owner
Located and purchased merchandise for jointly owned antique shop. Extensive travel to attend auctions and estate sales and visit architectural salvage firms.

• Education

B.A. Interior Design Quincy College

References Available

MARTIN FEINSTEIN

4111 BREMMERTON ROAD
ANAHEIM, CA 92803
714-555-8766
MARTINFEINSTEIN@XXX.COM

GOAL

Seeking challenging construction management projects.

EXPERTISE

Extensive experience in general construction, including institutional, commercial, and custom-built residential projects. Competent in all phases of general contracting and subcontracting. Experienced in securing financing, zoning, and building permits. Accurate cost estimating. Successful job bidding and contract negotiations.

EMPLOYERS

Since 2001 Owner, Feinstein Builders
1999-2001 Supervisor, ABC Construction
1997-1999 Safety Inspector, Warner Home Builders
1995-1997 Apprentice, Warner Home Builders

SAMPLE PROJECTS

- St. Mary's Church, rectory repair/remodeling
- Rosa's Cage, restaurant remodeling/expansion
- Hillside Shopping Center, outlet mall construction
- Green Grocery, prototype design for new food chain

EDUCATION

B.A. 1997 Business Administration
University of California, Davis

Course work in Building Trades
California Industrial Institute

Licensed Safety Inspector
State of California

REFERENCES

Available Upon Request

Arthur M. Hazelton, AIA

422 Casey Drive
Cambridge, MA 02238
(617) 555-4207
arthurhazelton@xxx.com

Services Offered

- On-site safety inspections
- Site selection and preparation
- Contract administration and fee negotiation
- Drafting, design, and project specifications
- Space planning
- Project management

Employment

2002-Present
Self-Employed Architect

Clients have included commercial and residential builders nationwide. Projects range from high-rise construction to multi-unit residential project. Arrange all project details from conception to financing to construction. Hire and supervise subcontractors. Negotiate bids and finalize contracts. Monitor progress of projects, and provide clients with ongoing verbal and written status reports.

Achievements

Redesign/remodel of 5,000-square-foot Trisco Cookie Factory
Analyzed production process. Redesigned plant layout to increase productivity. Upgraded equipment and fixtures.

Redesign/expansion of Clareton Condominiums
Supervised 4,000-square-foot expansion of condominium complex. Added four new units, increasing occupancy rate by 50 percent. Project completed on time and $10,000 under budget.

Employment (cont.)
1994-2002
Project Architect, In-house

Employers Included:
Winston and Strong, AIA: (617) 555-8122
Shepard Design Group: (617) 555-4423
Larrabe Construction: (617) 555-3212
Primose Design: (617) 555-1914

Education
Bachelor of Architecture   University of Virginia, 1992
Master of Architecture   University of New Hampshire, 1994

Affiliations
Member and current President of American Institute of Architects
New England Architectural Society
Licensed, Virginia and Massachusetts

References Available

Mark Donohue

6804 Scannell Road
St. Louis, MO 63146

Phone: (314) 555-5968
Markdonohue@xxx.com

Complete Interior Design

Creative space-saving solutions
Energy-efficient materials and designs
Unified interior and landscape design
Unique architectural detailing

Recent Clients

Martin Colby Furniture, Design Consultant
Designed furniture groupings on showroom floor.
Assisted with front window dressing.

Drexler Corporate Plaza, Design Management
Complete interior design for 50-room corporate office.
Selection of furnishings, color schemes, and floor layouts.
Supervision of contractors.

Roadside Inn, Interior Design
Redesign of hotel's kitchen and restaurant area.
Upgraded all fixtures and appliances.
Designed a 1,000-square-foot expansion of the dining area.

Education

B.A. in Interior Design
Rhode Island School of Design

References

Reference list and portfolio available.

Candice Selby

877 W. Grove Street
Miami, Florida 33152
(305) 555-9505
(305) 555-1889
candiceselby@xxx.com

Background

Seeking part-time drafting position, with potential for full-time employment following completion of Bachelor of Architecture degree

Expertise

Drafting
Computer Design
Site Inspection
Surveying
Skilled Carpentry

Employers

Homes & Smith, AIA
Drafter
2000 to Present

Dugan Designs
Drafter
1997-2000

Lewis Construction Inc.
Carpenter's Assistant
1994-1997

Education

Miami Central Community College
Associate's Degree
Drafting, 1994

Florida State University
B. Arch. Program
Anticipated graduation date: June 2004

References

References and work samples available

NANCY MILLIGAN
426 Hartford Lane
Pittsfield, MA 01203
(413) 555-7665
nancymilligan@xxx.com

EMPLOYMENT
Owner
Milligan Interiors, Pittsfield, MA
2001-Present
Own and manage interior design business. Purchase fine furnishings and manage
staff of two salespeople and one assistant designer. Assist clients in selecting and
coordinating purchases. Supervise daily operations.

Columnist
Pittsfield Gazette, Pittsfield
1999-Present
Write weekly column "Accent on Design," offering decorating tips in response to
readers' letters.

Design Consultant
Prestige Design, Boston
1995-1999
Interior designer for firm specializing in office remodeling/redecorating projects.
Visited clients on-site to plan design. Developed budgets and design sketches for
client approval.

Sales Associate
Expressions, Pittsfield
1993-1995
Customer service for furniture store. Assisted customers in selecting furniture,
coordinating fabrics and finishes with existing pieces.

CREDENTIALS
B.A./Interior Design
Rhode Island School of Design, 1993
Member, AISA

REFERENCES AVAILABLE

MANUEL CRUZE   Manuelcruze@xxx.com

532 N. Lynwood Court   St. Michaels, MD 21652

                                          Telephone: 410-555-3409

                                          Pager: 419-555-1130

CREDENTIALS

B. Arch. University of Maryland, 2002

3.5 G.P.A. Financed 75 percent of education through part-time employment in building trades. Winner of McIntyre Architectural Scholarship and Senior Design Award.

License: #R-6877, issued by State of Maryland, 2003

SKILLS

CAD/CAM design experience
Specifications writing
On-site project management
Fluent in Spanish

EMPLOYERS

Robinson Design Group
St. Michaels, MD
May 1999 to Present
Architectural Draftsman

Carlson Associates
Baltimore, MD
June 1996 to April 1999
Design Assistant

R.T.W. Construction
Baltimore, MD
Summers, 1994-1996
Construction Worker

REFERENCES

Available Upon Request

DAVID YUKIMURA

7802 Kiluea Road • Kiluea, HI 96743

Davidyukimura@xxx.com • 808-555-7584

BACKGROUND

Licensed architect specializing in real estate development, project and facilities management, and architectural design.

EMPLOYMENT HISTORY

7/99 to Present   **Garden Island Builders**
Project Architect   **Kauai, Hawaii**

Create and review schematic drawings for industrial and residential construction projects. Inspect and report on existing building conditions. Select building sites. Develop project schedules and budgets; secure financing; create construction specifications, blueprints, and models.

6/95 to 6/99   **Farley and White, AIA**
Architectural Designer   **Honolulu, Hawaii**

Responsible for all phases of interior construction and facilities management, including space layout and supervision of subcontractors. Created architectural remodeling designs for residential building clients. Responsible for materials procurement, contract negotiations, and creation of design specs.

4/96 to 6/99   **Sharpe Design Limited**
Project Coordinator   **Boston, Massachusetts**

Developed project guidelines and established budgets and deadlines for corporate design projects. Served as client representative in bidding and contract negotiations with subcontractors. Created construction specifications and documentation. Reviewed blueprints and schematic drawings.

1/94 to 4/96   **Quality Builders**
Research Assistant   **Boston, Massachusetts**

Responsible for project sketches and documentation. Created feasibility studies and scale models.

CREDENTIALS

Registered Architect, Boston and Hawaii

B. Arch./M. Arch. Massachusetts Institute of Technology

Member, American Institute of Architects

Member, American Home Builders Association

REFERENCES

Will be provided upon request.

James Price

855 Oakdale Road
Cleveland, OH 44115
(216) 555-8766
jamesprice@xxx.com

OBJECTIVE
Position as draftsman, with opportunity for growth.

EMPLOYERS
Walter S. Thompson Associates, Cleveland
Architectural Draftsman, 2001 to Present

- Responsible for drafting projects of all sizes. Prepare schematic drawings and scale models for diverse clients, ranging from large commercial enterprises to quaint private homes. Assist architects with accurate preparation of construction documents.

M & R Architectural Group, Indianapolis
Architectural Assistant, 1999 to 2001

- Prepared appropriate documentation to secure zoning and building permits in a timely fashion. Researched title and land law. Assisted in preparation and presentation of client proposals.

Worthington Design, Indianapolis
Office Manager, 1996 to 1999

- Managed daily office functions for large interior design firm. Completed commended design sketches and scale models for clients' review. Created and maintained a variety of documents and databases. Streamlined office functions. Acted as liaison between designers, clients, and suppliers.

EDUCATION
Peterskill Design Institute, New York
Associate's Degree
Drafting/Design
Graduated 1996

REFERENCES
Personal and professional references available

Gregory Cruze

3160 Richardson Street
Fayetteville, New York 13066
(315) 555-8314
gregorycruze@xxx.com

Architectural Experience

1999 to Present
R. S. Kent & Associates/Architects, Inc., Fayetteville, NY
Responsibilities: Draftsman, surveyor, assistant to project architects

1996 to 1999
Design Works, Inc., Park Ridge, IL
Responsibilities: Draftsman, designer, carpenter

1994 to 1996
Lewis & Landau, Inc., Corvallis, OR
Responsibilities: Draftsman, office manager

Education

University of Colorado
Drafting Technology Certificate
1994

Syracuse University
College of Architecture
Projected graduation date: May 2004

References Available upon Request

MICHAEL BEYER

—*m*—

9009 Bednar Road • Gurnee, IL 60031
(847) 555-8751 • michaelbeyer@xxx.com

—*m*—

EXPERIENCE

Fourteen years of experience in city planning, home inspection, building trades, and project management.

—*m*—

WORK HISTORY

March 2000 to Present
City of Gurnee
Zoning Commissioner

Manage all aspects of zoning and urban planning for the city. Facilitate zoning meetings, review building requests from new businesses, make recommendations to mayor's office, and issue zoning permits. Coordinate with Department of Community Development on long-term planning issues. Supervise staff of four.

June 1999 to March 2000
Archer Home Services, Home Inspector

Conducted on-site inspections of new and previously owned homes for buyers. Investigated structural integrity of properties; tested appliances, heating and cooling systems, and water pressure. Issued written reports of property status, including suggestions for repairs as needed.

—m—

WORK HISTORY (CONT.)

May 1997 to May 1999
Perkins Lumber, Manager

Manager of home improvement store. Provided customer service and advice on building procedures and materials. Supervised sales staff of 10. Reported to general manager. Responsible for all aspects of daily store management.

—m—

TRAINING

Completed three-year apprenticeship in building trades sponsored by Ryerson Technical Institute. Course work included courses in carpentry, business management, and home inspection.

Member, International Conference of Building Inspectors (ICBO)

Certified Building Inspector, State of Illinois

References are available.

LEE ALLEN TRENT, AIA

416 ELM STREET • COLUMBUS, OHIO 44020
614-555-4655 • LEETRENT@XXX.COM

OBJECTIVE   Position as a project architect with growing, dynamic firm

SUMMARY
- Proven client relations and management abilities; successfully train and motivate staff
- Superior written and verbal communications skills; create successful client proposals
- Project management experience; able to manage several concurrent projects and conclude each on time and within budget

JOB HISTORY   Project Manager, Winston and Stern
Columbus, Ohio, 2001-Present

Supervise draftsman, interns, and administrative assistant. Complete responsibility for commercial construction and remodeling projects, including site selection, surveying, preparation of bid specifications, permit and zoning permissions, contract approval, and financing.

Design Architect, Crosscurrents Design
Chicago, Illinois, 1999-2001

Responsible for drafting, blueprint development, space planning, and design for interior design firm specializing in large residential developments. Coordinated work of designers, architects, and subcontractors.

Draftsman, TDK Construction
Evanston, Illinois, 1996-1999

Responsible for creation of blueprints and scale models, surveying work, and on-site inspections.

Page 1 of 2

EDUCATION

B. Arch.
Northwestern University, Evanston, Illinois, 1999

LICENSE

Illinois #R6211

REFERENCES

Sam Lewis
Owner, TDK Construction
4820 Ridge Avenue
Evanston, Illinois 60646
847-555-2416
samlewis@xxx.com

Karen Politz
Designer, Crosscurrents Design
8319 Wellington Court, Ste. 112
Chicago, Illinois 60687
312-555-3948
karenpolitz@xxx.com

Paul W. Perez, AIA

---

433 Ashland Avenue • Lowell, MI 49503 • 616-555-8987

Goal

Seeking position with nationally known architectural firm where I can use and enhance my skills in all phases of architecture and design.

Skills

Managerial Ability: On-site supervision of labor. Coordination and scheduling of work done by all principals, including architects, engineers, investors, owners, lawyers, and inspectors.

Financial Skills: Cost estimating and accounting, contract negotiations.

Technical Abilities: Drafting, skilled carpentry, AutoCAD design.

Sample Projects: Design Consultant, Lowell Municipal Library
Project Manager, First National Bank remodeling
Project Manager, Sierra Café
Draftsman, Lemont Towers Condominium Construction

Employers

Quest Construction, Grand Rapids, MI
Project Architect 2002-Present

Morgan Design Group, Grand Rapids, MI
Design Draftsman 1998-2002

Education

B. Arch. University of Michigan, Ann Arbor, MI 2001
M.S. Arch. University of Michigan, anticipated date of completion: June 2004

Affiliations

Licensed by the State of Illinois, #T-8755
Member, American Institute of Architects, Michigan Chapter, since 2001

References

List of references and portfolio are available.

Nicholas Vittico

832 Hillside Drive
Brooklyn, New York 10036
212-555-8756
nicholasvittico@xxx.com

Goal

Entry-level job as drafter for a local architectural firm

Education

Associate Degree, Drafting
Allerton School of Design—2002
- Maintained G.P.A. of 3.5
- Earned 80 percent of tuition

Graduate
McMurray Technical High School—1998
- Voted Outstanding Senior by teachers and classmates

Employment

Construction Worker, Benson & Sons
2000 to present
- Worked construction jobs during summer for four years
- Operated heavy equipment
- Delivered building materials to job sites
- Achieved rank of junior carpenter

References Will Be Provided Upon Request

James Jackson

4217 E. Washington Street
St. Louis, MO 63119
314-555-9487
jamesjackson@xxx.com

Summary

Qualified for skilled carpentry positions of all kinds. Experienced in rough and finished carpentry, woodworking, and furniture design and construction.

Education

Graduate, Local 7, International Carpenters Union Apprenticeship Program
Graduate, Lincoln Vocational High School

Job Experience

2002-Present
Draftsman, Belle Architectural Inc., St. Louis, MO
- Responsible for drafting and blueprint reading and construction of scale models for architects.

1999-2002
Assistant Manager, Blair Woodworking, Columbus, MO
- Assisted owner of precision woodworking shop with design and production of custom furniture. Worked on special-order projects for homeowners and builders.

References

Business and personal references on request. Detailed photo portfolio available.

Clara Preston, AIA

Phone: 617-555-3498 • E-mail: clarapreston@xxx.com
3215 Rockingham Road • Boston, MA 02151
License #S-9877 • State of Massachusetts

Work History

1999-Present
Preston Architectural Services
> Self-employed architectural and engineering consultant handling a wide variety of projects. Examples: Clearwater Bed and Breakfast (a 15-room country inn) and Benton School of Music (5,000 sq. ft. music school with three acres of landscaped grounds).

1997-1999
Smith and Holt, Inc.
> Project architect for mid-size architectural firm involved in industrial design and construction projects. Responsible for contract negotiations, preparation of client proposals, job bidding, and field supervision on both commercial and residential projects.

1995-1997
Remington Industries, Inc.
> Engineering design consultant for architectural firm specializing in large-scale industrial construction. Responsible for cost estimating, feasibility testing, and space planning. Created block layouts, test layouts, and stacking plans.

Credentials

B. Arch. Boston College
M. Arch. MIT

References Available

RAYMOND R. WILLIAMSON

42 Deerpath Drive • Fayetteville, New York 13066
(315) 555-5959 • (315) 555-5400 (cell)
raymondwilliamson@xxx.com

GOAL

Responsible position in architectural design and construction with nationally known firm that rewards personal initiative and innovative design.

SKILLS

Space Planning
Materials Selection
Design Specification
Cost Estimating
Contract Negotiations
Fee Negotiations
Field Observation
Client Relations

HISTORY

Partner, Williamson & Reade, Inc., 2001-Present
Project Architect, Klein Associates, 1999-2001
Drafter/Designer, Wyler Group, 1997-1999

PROJECTS

Keller Eye Clinic, construction
The Tree House, retail remodeling
Oakhurst Mall, food court design
Walker Junior High, repair/remodeling
Tiny Tots Daycare, playground design

EDUCATION

B. Arch., Syracuse University, 1996

LICENSE

State of New York, No. S-9087

REFERENCES

Available on Request

Morris G. Parker

502 Western Avenue
Denver, CO 80200
(303) 555-9878
morrisparker@xxx.com

Professional Goal

To use my drafting skills and knowledge of building trades to assist an architectural or construction firm in the creation of quality housing.

Employment History

Design Draftsman
Pioneer Log Homes Inc.
June 1999 to Present
Denver, Colorado

> Create blueprints and specifications for prefabricated housing supplier. Recommend materials, create layouts, and troubleshoot technical problems. Housing built is energy efficient, durable, and affordable.

Construction Supervisor
McClean Builders
May 1997 to June 1999
Boulder, Colorado

> Supervised construction crews on-site for residential builder. Trained new hires; scheduled employees and subcontractors. Ensured compliance with safety procedures. Guaranteed control. Monitored progress and issued status reports.

Roofer
Crawford Construction
September 1995 to May 1997
Denver, Colorado

> Installed roofs for local home builder firm. Worked part-time while completing degree.

Education

Denver Technical Institute
Building Trades Program
Certificate of Completion, 1995

References Available

Daniel Sullivan

250 Brady Street
Cleveland, Ohio 44115
(216) 555-4958
danielsullivan@xxx.com

Background

Licensed electrician with 15 years' experience as contactor/subcontractor
for a wide variety of commercial, residential, and industrial projects.

Credentials

Ohio License C-46237
Certified by Cleveland Technical College Apprenticeship Program

Skills

Supervise crews of 2 to 12 people as on-site foreman
Train apprentice and journeyman electricians
Ensure safety and quality control on-site
Purchase materials and equipment
Estimate costs
Coordinate with architects, building inspectors, contractors, and
  subcontractors
Complete wiring for a wide variety of projects, including hospital, nuclear
  power plant, shopping mall, and apartment complex

Employers

The DiAngelo Company
Master Electrician
2000-Present

Citizens Electric
General Foreman
1996-2000

Cleveland Light
Journeyman Electrician
1994-1996

References Available Upon Request

BARBARA WILSON

2440 N. THIRD STREET • TULSA, OK 74101
(918) 555-9868 • barbarawilson@xxx.com

PROFESSIONAL EXPERIENCE

Environmental Testing

Collect and analyze samples to assess air quality and water pollution. Inspect suspected sites of pollution and issue status reports and recommendations.

Urban Planning

Consult with city and county governments on community development. Inspect sites for new and expanding communities. Ensure compliance with municipal building codes once projects are under way.

Land Management

Responsible for stream and timber management. Conduct educational tours of wetlands. Create topographical maps.

EMPLOYED BY

City of Tulsa, Department of Community Development
Job Title: Urban Planning Consultant
Dates: June 1999 to Present

Oklahoma Environmental Agency
Job Title: Public Health Inspector
Dates: May 1996 to April 1999

Washington State Bureau of Land Management
Job Title: Environmental Engineer
Dates: January 1992 to May 1996

EDUCATION

B.S. University of Colorado 1992
Major: Environmental Studies
Minor: Chemistry

REFERENCES

Available on Request

Justin Keaton, AIA

2416 Vicory Road
Arlington, VA 22202
(703) 555-5958
justinkeaton@xxx.com

Experienced, talented architect seeking employment with established firm dedicated to urban planning and renewal

Work History

2000-Present: Project architect for Harrison and Packard Inc.
Responsibilities include:
Creating and presenting initial and final plans, blueprints, and proposals to superiors, clients, and municipal boards
Supervising two junior associates

1999-2000: Specification writer for Snyder Architectural Inc.
Responsibilities included:
Interpreting architectural plans for builders
Writing project proposals

1994-1999: Draftsman for Grant Design Associates
Responsibilities included:
Producing architectural drawings
Creating scale models

Credentials

Bachelor of Architecture, Brown University, 1994
Licensed by State of Virginia, 1995

References are available.

MIRANDA GOLDBERT

411 Archer Street   Gradyville, PA 19039
(610) 555-5904   mirandagoldbert@xxx.com

OWNER

Petunia's Nursery, Established 1998

- Responsible for all aspects of managing successful landscaping/ nursery business.
- Manage staff of eight.
- Interview, hire, train, schedule, and supervise employees.
- Purchase merchandise.
- Select and procure wide variety of annual and perennial flowers, vegetables and herbs, and trees and shrubs. Responsible for all budgeting and inventory control.
- Assist clients with landscape design.
- Design/redesign gardens and landscapes to client specifications. Offer maintenance training sessions or packages.
- Conduct regular follow-up assessments.

AWARDS/ACTIVITIES

Winner, Best Floral Design
Country Gardens Magazine, 2001

Winner, Business Woman of the Year
Gradyville Chamber of Commerce, 1999

President, Gradyville Gardening Club, 1997

FORMER EMPLOYERS

Blossoms, Floral Designer 1995-1997
Lowe's Nursery, Assistant Manager 1994-1995
Thompson's Stitchery, Salesperson 1992-1994

EDUCATION

B.A. in Landscape Design from Stevens College, 1992

References Available

KEN NIELSEN

190 Hazelton Road
Cambridge, MA 02140
(617) 555-3948
kennielsen@xxx.com

SUMMARY

Experienced contractor
Owner of successful construction firm
Skilled carpenter
Trained professional with strong work ethic
Fluent in Spanish

PROJECTS

- Design and construction/remodeling or repair
- Patios–decks–gazebos–porches–greenhouses
- Design and build additions to homes, assisting homeowner with planning and procuring materials

EMPLOYMENT RECORD

Owner, Nielsen Exteriors 1998-Present
- Use carpentry skills to assist residential builder with remodeling projects. Responsibilities include drawing and interpreting plans and acquiring permits. Hire subcontractor and schedule and supervise work to guarantee adherence to schedules and building codes.

CREDENTIALS

Cambridge Community College
Carpenter Apprenticeship Program
Completed 1996

University of Massachusetts
Entrepreneurial Management Seminar Series
Completed 1998

MEMBER

American Home Builders Association

REFERENCES

Provided on Request

Richard Taylor

3923 Montgomery Road
Louisville, Kentucky 94229
Phone: 502-555-5422
Richardtaylor@xxx.com

OBJECTIVE	Opportunity to assist an architectural or construction firm with the challenges of successful fiscal management
SKILLS	Productivity Studies Inventory Control Cost Estimating Budgeting Auditing Quality Control
EMPLOYERS	President, Taylor Business Consultants July 2001 to Present Budget Analyst, Charleton Architects Inc. May 1999 to June 2001 Financial Planner, Preston Financial January 1995 to May 1999
EDUCATION	University of Virginia, B.S., 1994 Accounting Major
REFERENCES	Available

GEORGE L. RICHARDS

802 Crest Avenue
Dubuque, Iowa 52001
Phone: 319-555-4857
Georgerichards@xxx.com

SUMMARY

Ten years of experience: five as self-employed general contractor and five as journeyman plumber. Specialized training in solar heating, plumbing, and drafting.

EMPLOYMENT

Richards Construction, Owner
October 1999-Present

General contractor working on residential rehabilitation and remodeling projects. Install heating systems, both solar and conventional. Install plumbing systems. Hire subcontractors for electrical, roofing, and other specialized work. Supervise subcontractors on-site to ensure quality control and compliance with deadlines.

Keegan Plumbing, Journeyman Plumber
September 1994-October 1999

On-the-job training with local plumbing firm through plumbing apprenticeship program. Subsequently hired as journeyman plumber. Installed plumbing systems. Handled service calls.

EDUCATION

Drafting course, University of Iowa, 1994

Plumbing apprenticeship program, Washington Community College, 1992-1994

Industrial training on solar heating systems, ITT Technical College, 1993

REFERENCES AVAILABLE

SANDRA JONES

850 Princeton Road
Bethesda, MD 20014
301-555-9032
301-555-9438
sandrajones@xxx.com

GOAL

Opportunity to assist an architectural firm or a construction company with the challenges of project management

EMPLOYMENT HISTORY

Jason Construction, Project Manager, 2001-Present
- Coordinate building projects for residential construction firm. Hire and supervise architects and subcontractors. Prepare all necessary documents, including contracts and permit applications. Negotiate financing.

Bethesda Department of Housing, Real Estate Analyst, 1993-2001
- Gathered and analyzed demographic and housing statistics. Designed census and questionnaire to assess area vacancy rates, housing needs, and displacement patterns. Wrote comprehensive reports and recommendations regarding property management.

EDUCATION

B.A. Urban Studies
University of Virginia 1993

REFERENCES

Available

Carl Brinkman

Address
1011 Crystal Drive
Berkeley, CA 94707

Phone
(415) 555-8609 Home
(415) 555-8797 Cell

E-mail
Carlbrinkman@xxx.com

Objective

Community development position for mid-size nonprofit or governmental agency.

Assets

Committed to creation of quality low-cost housing
B.A. in Sociology and M.A. in Urban Planning
Excellent fund-raising and grant-writing skills
Experienced relocation counselor

Job History

Program Director
Berkeley Community Development Association
1997-Present

Research community development issues for City Council and Urban Planning Commission, including:
- Vacancy Rates
- Mortgage Rates and Availability
- Business Relocation Needs
- Land Transfer Law

Relocation Specialist
Urban Housing Commission
1997-1999

Designed relocation strategies with input from community leaders and business investors. Directed fund-raising initiatives. Wrote grant proposals.

Job History (cont.)

Relocation Counselor
Urban Housing Commission
1995-1997

Informed residents of their rights and responsibilities during housing conversion and eviction procedures. Offered community referral services. Educated residents on options, eligibility for housing assistance, and low-income mortgage projects.

Education

M.A. in Urban Planning
University of California at Sacramento

B.A. in Sociology
San Jose State University

References

Available

PAUL HAMILTON

621 Courtney Lane • Baltimore, MD 21218

Paulhamilton@xxx.com • Telephone (410) 555-1897

OBJECTIVE

Self-expression and professional service through creative, hands-on interior design and educational endeavors in the decorative arts.

EXPERIENCE

Interior design
Creative floor plans
Functional design details
Coordinated fabrics and furnishings
Knowledgeable restoration, period details
Personalized color schemes and textile designs
Communications
Interior design instruction
Photojournalism
Landscape design
Coordinated landscape and interior design
Expert plant selection and maintenance advice
Creative outdoor "rooms"

EMPLOYERS

Hamilton Community College
Instructor, Principles of Interior Design
2002-Present

Interior Design
Contributing Editor
1996-Present

Ivy Productions, Landscape and Interior Design
Decorator
1999-2002

Madden Textiles
Fabric Designer
1997-1999

CREDENTIALS

B.A. Decorative Arts
North Park College 1996
Member, ASIA

REFERENCES

Ivy Grant, Owner
Ivy Productions
410-555-9087
ivygrant@xxx.com

Leo Thomson, Editor
Interior Design magazine
410-555-0877
leothomson@xxx.com

Michael Madden, President
Madden Textiles
410-555-3847
michealmadden@xxx.com

PORTFOLIO AVAILABLE

Manuel King

412 Westminster
Denver, CO 80030
303-555-3100
manuelking@xxx.com

Strengths

✓ Skilled equipment and furnishings selection
✓ Successful contract administration
✓ Creative space planning, color and texture specifications
✓ Articulate and professional client presentations
✓ Experienced engineering liaison

Recent Projects

Interior Design Consultant 2001
Denver Public Schools, Denver, CO
Provided design services, including space planning and furniture and equipment selection, for five schools. Supervised installation on-site.

Design Engineer 1999
Weston Exhibits Inc., Boulder, CO
Created design and specifications for trade exhibit manufacturer. Selected colors and finishes for exhibits. Developed assembly instructions.

Project Manager 1996-1999
Westdale Condominiums, Westminster, CO
Directed condominium-remodeling project. Created design drawings. Maintained budgets, schedules, and all documentation. Completed project featured in *Southwest Design*, August 1998 issue.

Education

B.A. Interior Design
University of California, Davis 1996

References & Portfolio Available

PENNY RYAN

566 Grove Street • Park Ridge, IL 60068
(847) 555-8576
pennyryan@xxx.com

SKILLS

- Drafting
- Skilled Carpentry
- Design and Construction Document Preparation
- Office Management

EMPLOYERS

Thomas Tipton and Associates, Chicago
2002 to Present

ATS Architectural Group, Park Ridge
1999 to 2002

Design Works, Inc., St. Paul
1997 to 1999

EDUCATION

University of Illinois
B.S./Architectural Technology
June 1996

St. Paul Community College
A.S./Drafting & Design
June 1997

REFERENCES

Warren Wright, Architect
Thomas Tipton Associates
312-555-2354, ext. 401

Claire Baxter, Architect
ATS Architectural Group
708-555-9886

Sandra Keller

316 Third Street
Atlanta, GA 64381
(404) 555-6579
sandrakeller@xxx.com

SUMMARY

Ten years of experience in all phases of general contracting and subcontracting
Excellent record of meeting target deadlines and budgets
Effective management and client relations skills
Creative solutions to mechanical and space-planning challenges

STRUCTURES BUILT

855 Dobbs Road, 50,000-square-foot factory
4611 Hunter Parkway, 40-unit apartment complex
622 Charleston Place, 20-unit condominium development
Warren Road & Highway 66, The Courtyard housing development

EMPLOYERS

T. J. Duncan & Company 1999-Present
Project Manager
Duties include establishing budgets and schedules, soliciting bids from subcontractors and finalizing contracts, and preparing and presenting preliminary sketches and scale models to clients.

Richardson Construction 1996-1999
Surveyor
Responsible for establishing construction site, determining lot lines, and creating maps and sketches as necessary. Researched survey and land record laws for superiors. Wrote property descriptions.

Evans & Sons 1996-1999
General Laborer
Handled general construction duties for home builder. Operated heavy machinery. Delivered materials to job sites.

EDUCATION
Atlanta Junior College
Certified, Land Surveyor 1997

Apprenticeship
Georgia Building Development Association 1998

REFERENCES WILL BE PROVIDED UPON REQUEST.

■ ANNE PERKINS

423 Royalton Court
Monterey, CA 90766
E-mail anneperkins@xxx.com
Telephone 202-555-9686

■ GOAL

Further professional experience in design, architecture, and historical preservation.

■ ASSETS

Extensive knowledge of interior design, architecture, and preservation
Excellent supervisor
Good organization skills
Effective fund-raiser
Competent communicator

■ AREAS OF EXPERTISE

DESIGN

■ Created interior designs for 20 model homes in five locations statewide for a major residential builder. Responsible for color schemes, space planning, furniture selection, and window treatments.

■ Completed all designs to supervisor's satisfaction. All work completed on time and within budget.

BUSINESS MANAGMENT

■ Successfully recruited and trained group of 12 volunteers for San Francisco Preservation Council.

■ Developed standard office procedures for Robinson & Associates, an architectural firm. Generated and maintained all project documents, contracts, and client files.

■ Developed and executed direct-mail campaign that raised $40,000 for San Francisco Preservation Council.

■ PROFESSIONAL HISTORY

Director
San Francisco Preservation Council
June 2001-Present

Designer
Lexington Builders
May 1999-June 2001

Office Manager
Robinson & Associates
January 1996-April 1999

■ EDUCATION

San Francisco City College
B.S. Accounting 1996

University of California, L.A.
B.A. Interior Design 1994

References Available

MARY YATES

748 Lewis Parkway
Morristown, New Jersey 07869
201-555-5955 (Home)
201-555-4059 (Work)
maryyates@xxx.com

BACKGROUND

Executive assistant to architectural firm. Excellent communication, problem solving, and client relations skills. Able to meet tight deadlines, mediate disputes, and work under pressure.

PROFESSIONAL EXPERIENCE

R.K. Winston Associates
Office Administrator 1999-Present

Coordinate all aspects of industrial high-rise construction projects. Monitor progress and issue status reports to supervisors and investors. Originate and maintain all documentation. Conduct weekly status meetings between architects and subcontractors.

Davis & Davis Construction
Executive Secretary 1997-1999

Assisted president of commercial construction firm with document preparation, work scheduling, and office management. Monitored work of subcontractors and informed supervisor of project status.

Rolland, Regis, & Harp, Attorneys
Legal Assistant 1995-1997

Assisted attorneys with client interactions and document preparation, including all contracts and depositions.

EDUCATION

Associate's Degree
Brookside Business College 1994

MEMBERSHIPS

Executive Secretaries International
Women in Business

REFERENCES

Will be provided upon request

Kevin Price

884 Lincoln Circle • Los Gatos, CA 95030
Kevinprice@xxx.com

Goal

To expand my experience and knowledge of architectural design and construction.

Employment History

2000-Present
Price Architectural Design Inc.
Owner

Commercial and residential remodeling and construction projects for wide range of clients.

- Space planning, materials, selection, and installation for 50-unit condo complex.

- Redesign of Walker Dental Clinic to provide three additional examination areas and a larger waiting room.

- Design and construction of Secret Garden, café and gourmet food store

1998-2000
Stein and Associates
Project Architect

Project architect for large local firm. Position included fee negotiations and developing design specifications, schematics, and scale models as needed.

- Maintenance and repair work at Central High School, including inspection and documentation of existing conditions and supervision of all repairs necessary to bring mechanicals up to code.

- Redesign and upgrading of Emergency Room at Stevenson Memorial, from design through construction observation.

Education

Bachelor of Architecture
University of Hawaii at Manoa 1995

Certification
AutoCAD R-11

Registration

Registered Architect
California No. 8767 1995

References available

ALFRED FOSTER

622 Foxfire Lane
Bellevue, WA 98007
Telephone 206-555-7655
Alfredfoster@xxx.com

OBJECTIVE

Continued opportunity for professional development in the field of architecture as I work toward becoming a licensed architect

EXPERIENCE

Contractor
Wilson Bishop, AIA 2001-Present
Freelance architectural draftsman/site inspector on long-term contract basis with Bellevue architectural firm specializing in residential development projects.

Draftsman
Williamson and Lewis, 1999-2001
Prepared documents and scale models as needed for construction and remodeling projects, under the supervision of Seattle architects Williamson and Lewis.

Junior Draftsman
Hinkley Design, 1996-1999
Created variety of working drawings as entry-level draftsman for Seattle design firm.

EDUCATION

Full-time architectural student
University of Washington
Anticipated date of graduation is June 2004.

References and work samples available upon request.

MIGDALIA MOLINA

414 Casey Court, #201
Baton Rouge, LA 70802
Migdaliamolina@xxx.com

EDUCATION	B. Arch., LSU, School of Architecture, 1990
AWARDS & ACTIVITIES	LSU Merit Award Howell Merit Scholarship Carmichael Theatre Restoration Project Habitat for Humanity
PROFESSIONAL EXPERIENCE	Gould Design Group, Baton Rouge 5/98 to Present Drafter/Designer Davidson Associates, Lafayette 8/95 to 5/98 Architectural Assistant Star Construction, Boulder, CO 1992 to 1995 Summers Carpentry Assistant
SKILLS	Computer Design/Drafting Scale Model Construction Specifications Writing Field Experience Fluent in Spanish

References Available

BARBARA THOMAS, AIA

1902 Elm Street • Kalamazoo, MI 46302
614-555-6412 • barbarathomas@xxx.com

OBJECTIVE

Opportunities to revitalize communities through application of my urban planning and architectural skills.

ACHIEVEMENTS

- Fifteen years of experience as an urban planner/architect
- Creator of successful rehabilitation projects in troubled and underdeveloped urban neighborhoods
- Effective liaison between government agencies, contractors, and neighborhood leaders
- Responsible urban planner, developing concurrent efforts to create low-cost housing and commercial properties—an approach that encourages stability and growth in neighborhoods

WORK HISTORY

2000 to Present—Project Director
Jacobson and Associates
411 Kerrigan Road
Kalamazoo, MI 46302

Designed the $12 million Grady Street Housing Project in Detroit. Managed staff of six and coordinated work of all contractors, architects, legal counsel, and support staff involved. Project completed on time and $20,000 under budget.

1996 to 2000—Urban Designer
Starmont Design Inc.
2340 N. Warren Road
Carmel, IN 46032

Diverse experience in commercial property design. Responsible for design, planning, budgeting, and supervision. Liaison to corporate executives, city agencies, and legal counsel. Projects included retail and office spaces and community and civic centers. Successfully met tight deadlines and budgets.

Page 1 of 2

EDUCATION
Stanford University, B.S., Architecture, 1992
Syracuse University, M.S., Urban Design, 1996

AFFILIATIONS
American Institute of Architects
American Urban Planning Association

References Available

Alice Miller

42 Fenton Street

Aspen, Colorado 81612

(303) 555-9488

alicemiller@xxx.com

Objective
New design challenges and opportunities to enhance clients' work and home environments through creative interior design.

Skills
Landscape Design
Interior Design
Project Management

Projects
Interior Design, Nordic Chalet
Project included room design: selection of furnishings and flooring, wall coverings, linens, and artwork for 300-room ski chalet.

Space Planning/Design Consult, Nero Fitness Center
Designed floor plan for exercise, locker room, and snack bar areas. Selected design materials and color scheme.

Landscape Design, Fun Village
Created designs for all exterior areas of amusement park: entry arches and fountain, landscaping, rest areas, and outdoor food court.

Employers
Owner, Miller Design 2001 to Present
Design Associate, Creative Interiors 1999 to 2001
Assistant Designer, Contempo Fabrics 1995 to 1999

Education
B.A. Rhode Island School of Design 1994

References Available

Emma Marie Bekiswe

412 Sheridan Road
Middletown, CT 07457
203-555-1234
emmabekiswe@xxx.com

INTERIOR DESIGNER
STRENGTHS
- Cost-effective design strategies
- Successful contract negotiations
- Innovative use of light and color
- Polished client presentations
- Solid team player who works well with engineers and architects

RECENT PROJECTS
Interior Design Consultant, 1999
Creative Image, New Haven, CT
- Provided design services, including floor plans and equipment selection, for photography chain. Basic design modified and applied to four retail outlets. Supervised on-site installation.

Design Engineer, 1998
Manhattan Display Company, New York, NY
- Created design and specifications for point-of-purchase displays. Assisted clients with the selection of colors and finishes for displays. Developed assembly instructions.

Project Manager, 1997-1998
Westchester Studios, New Britain, CT
- Held full responsibility for office building remodeling project. Created design drawings. Maintained budgets, schedules, and all documentation. Completed project on time and 10 percent under budget.

EDUCATION
Bachelor of Art (with honors) Interior Design
Mills College, Oakland, CA
May 1997

REFERENCES AND PORTFOLIO AVAILABLE

ERIC JONES

78 E. Sadler Street • East Hampton, NY 11937
(212) 555-6902 • ericjones@xxx.com

EXPERIENCE

ARCHITECTURE
Ten years of service and growth with professional architectural firms

CONSTRUCTION
Eight years of experience in building trades, administration,
and project management

RECENT EMPLOYMENT

BUILDING PLANS EXAMINER
- Analyze and interpret building plans and specifications
- Confer with engineers, architects, contractors, builders and the public concerning interpretation of compliance to engineering and code requirements
- Perform field inspections as necessary to investigate compliance queries
- East Hampton Department of Public Works, Building Permits Division, October 2001 to present

PROJECT ARCHITECT
- Hamilton Lodge (resort and golf course) project and design development
- Vidalia Spa design administration and management
- Upton Place (community development) project design and development
- Klein Design, Inc., Guilford, CT, March 1998 to October 2001

DESIGN DRAFTSMAN
- Marketplace Office Complex tenant improvements
- Carrollton Inn (475-key hotel) design development/schematics
- Lincoln Square (shopping mall) design development
- Orlen Design Group, Middleville, NJ, October 1995 to March 1998

Page 1 of 2

—— CREDENTIALS ——

American Institute of Architects (AIA)
New York State Council

Licensed Architect, State of New York
R3609

International Conference of Building Officials (ICBO)
Certified Plans Examiner and Building Inspector

M.S. Arch. Syracuse University 1994
B. Arch. Syracuse University 1990

References and portfolio furnished on request

SCOTT W. CURTISS, AIA

450 Old Mill Lane
Boston, MA 02266
(617) 555-3958
scottcurtiss@xxx.com

EXPERTISE
Program Analysis, Space Planning, Project Coordination, Facilities Management

EXPERIENCE
9/01-Present
Hirshey & Pierce, Boston, Project Architect
- Develop and analyze schematics for commercial and residential projects. Analyze and verify building conditions. Outline project, establish preliminary budget, and prepare construction drawings and models.

ACHIEVEMENTS
- Successful schematic design concept for $250,000 remodeling of Oak Haven, a 10,000-square-foot outlet shopping mall comprised of seven stores.
- Resolution of logistical and mechanical issues in site plan for 2,000-square-foot expansion to Boston College Library, including below-ground parking facility, through analysis of cost, pedestrian and vehicular traffic flow, and ADA regulations.

1/00-8/01
Perez Architectural Services, Inc., Seattle, Architectural Designer/Consultant
- Coordinated all stages of interior construction, facilities management, and space layout for commercial projects. Assisted clients with architectural designs for tenant development and improvement. Set schedules and budget. Negotiated contracts. Selected materials and equipment. Wrote design specifications.

ACHIEVEMENTS
Successfully reduced budget for construction of Olympia Medical Clinic by 10 percent while meeting all original functional objectives. Added space saving design improvements and reduced materials costs.

EXPERIENCE (CONT.)

1/98-12/00
Schroeder Design, Inc., Madison, WI, Project Coordinator

- Established project objectives, schedules, and budgets for corporate/financial projects. Served as client liaison for bidding and contract negotiations with subcontractors. Prepared construction documents and contracts. Reviewed mechanicals. Prepared and presented schematic plans.

ACHIEVEMENTS

- Prepared sketches and plans for adaptive reuse of 4,000-square-foot elementary school, including installation of computer facilities and state-of-the-art audiovisual conferencing center.

9/96-1/98
Martin & Martin, AIA, Madison, WI, Architectural Research Assistant

- Assisted architects with project documentation. Prepared feasibility studies, schematic drawings, and scale models.

CREDENTIALS

Registered architect, Wisconsin, 1996

University of Wisconsin, Madison
Bachelor of Architecture, 1994

Boston College
Bachelor of Fine Arts, 1990

Member, American Institute of Architects

REFERENCES WILL BE PROVIDED UPON REQUEST.

Architect
Marcus Williams

331 Willowbrook Road
Woodside, CA 94062
213-555-6749
marcuswilliams@xxx.com

Goal

Opportunity to enhance design and construction of residential properties through position with mid-size architectural firm.

Experience

University of California, Irvine, CA 2001-Present
Teach courses in architectural history, drafting, and design. Curriculum development experience. University Planning Committee chair, 2002-2003.

Burdette Construction, Woodside, CA 2000-2001
Responsible for development of construction plans for firm handling $20 million worth of residential construction. Job included CAD-CAM design, drafting, blueprint development, and project management. Assisted in development of price quotes and written proposals for clients.

Quinn Design Consultants, Richmond, VA 1994-1999
Designed and constructed custom fine furniture for homes and businesses. Supervised installation as necessary. Assisted in evaluation and procurement of materials.

Education

B.S. Architecture, University of Virginia 1994

References are available on request.

Alexandra Scott

622 Osteen Street • Knoxville, TN 37950 • 615-555-5466 • alexandrascott@xxx.com

Goal

To acquire diversified experience in landscape design that will enable me to better serve clients.

Recent Projects

Landscape Designer for Redwood Inn, Knoxville
Design and execution of grounds for 30-room inn. Project included design of perennial garden, formal rose garden, fish pond, and fountain. Provided client with preliminary sketches, scale models, and detailed budget. Coordinated work of subcontractors.

Gardening Consultant to Home Base, Inc., Savannah
Consultant to this national chain of home-improvement stores. Assisted marketing and purchasing executives working to develop and promote their own line of lawn and garden care products.

Landscape Designer for DeVille Cafe, Knoxville
Redesign of front entryway and design and construction of outdoor eating area in collaboration with interior designer. Planned space, designed garden, and trained client in maintenance techniques.

Employment History

1999-Present
Self-employed landscape architect

1997-1999
Landscape designer, Sterling Garden Services, Knoxville

1996-1997
Manager, Savannah Nursery, Savannah

Credentials

Degree
University of Georgia, B.A.
Environmental Design, 1995

Memberships
American Institute of Landscape Design
Southern Design Council

Awards
Best Formal Garden
Southern Design Council Contest

References

References are available on request.

Client Relations • Project Management • Architectural Design

Kevin Goldberg, AIA

185 Edens Lane • Fort Lauderdale, FL 33340
(305) 555-8986 • kevingoldberg@xxx.com

• Employment

2000-Present
Self-employed Architectural/Engineering Consultant
• Offer full range of consulting and subcontracting services. Varied scope and clientele. Recent projects have included (1) design of Fairview Inn, 12-room luxury hotel with two-acre garden and (2) design consult on airport control tower at Miami International.

1992-2000
Senior Architect, Ashberry and Royalton
• Full range of responsibilities, including contract negotiations, preparation of client proposals, cost estimating, and field observation on large- and small-scale commercial and residential projects.

1985-1992
Engineering Design Consultant, Wexler Industries
• Materials and design consultant for architectural design firm specializing in commercial high-rise construction. Position included job bidding, materials selection, and space planning. Created block and test layouts and stacking plans.

• Credentials

American Institute of Architects (AIA)
Florida Architectural License #R3042
Bachelor's degree, Architecture, University of Maryland
Master's degree, Structural Engineering, MIT

References Available

Taran Bouge Redding-Gagne

152 Coroba Court, #8
Isla del Mar, CA 94062
415-555-6653
tarangagne@xxx.com

Summary

- Ten years of experience in interior and textile design
- Excellent record of meeting deadlines and budgets
- Skilled project manager
- Creative architectural details and design solutions

Project Highlights

North Star Inn
Interior Design Consultant

Supervised redecoration of 800-square-foot lobby. Collaborated with landscape designer to ensure smooth transition from hotel exterior to interior. Finished lobby featured in *Creative Interiors*, Fall 2001.

Designer Showcase Home, Spring 2000
Textile Designer

Selected all fabrics and window treatments. Original fabric designs created for Starfield Fabrics used throughout the home.

Employers

Zephyr Designs, Textile Designer, 1999-present
Creative Interiors, Editorial Board, 1997-present
Starfield Fabrics, Design Director, 1995-1997

Education

B.A. in Interior Design, California Arts Academy, Pasadena, 1994

REGINALD SMITH

1402 Winchester, No. 106
Chicago, IL 60645
(312) 555-8611
reginaldsmith@xxx.com

PROFESSIONAL SKILLS

Managerial
- Daily supervision of construction job sites
- Coordination of subcontractors, architects, engineers, city planners, building managers, and owners
- Contract negotiations

Financial
- Cost estimating
- Cost accounting

Technical
- Drafting
- Skilled carpentry

SAMPLE PROJECTS

Design and Supervision
Oak Park Medical Building
Complete overhaul of 30,000-square-foot addition to existing construction, plus extensive interior and exterior renovation. Work included EPA cleanup and upgrading electrical system.

Carpentry
Lincoln Towers
Extensive restructuring of apartment complex. Work included framing, drywall, doors, flooring, kitchens, and trim carpentry for 40 condominiums.

EMPLOYERS

Smith Construction, Owner & Operator, 2001 to Present
Warner Construction, Superintendent, 1997-2001
David Wright and Associates, Superintendent, 1990-1997

EDUCATION

Warrenville Vocational College, Warrenville, Ohio
Associate Degree, 1995

Simpson Construction, Warrenville, Ohio
Skilled Carpentry Apprenticeship, 1995-1997

North Park College, Chicago, Illinois
Continuing education courses in accounting and business management, ongoing

MEMBERSHIPS

Professional Builders of America
Illinois Building and Construction Trades Council

COMMUNITY SERVICE

Local sponsor, Habitat for Humanity
Board member, Mayor's Council on Recycling & Environmental Awareness

REFERENCES

Michael Morgan, President, Warner Construction (708) 555-9813

David Wright, CEO, David Wright & Associates (312) 555-9854

Sue Kamajura, Building Manager, Lincoln Towers (312) 555-4978

JAMES PEREZ

123 Oakdale Drive   Blue Springs, MD 64015
816-555-9997   jamesperez@xxx.com

BACKGROUND

Carpenter with eight years of experience, specializing in exterior foundation work in new homes; creation, construction, and installation of special-order furniture and cabinetry.

EXPERIENCE

Site Supervisor, White Oak Construction, Inc., 1998-Present
- Manage work of five carpenters on-site for established residential builder. Review and interpret blueprints. Supervise construction of wood foundations and addition of woodwork to existing foundations. Responsible for creating and adhering to work schedules and budgets.

Carpenter, Brownsberry Interiors, 1996-1998
- Created custom cabinets, shelving units, and furniture for architectural firm specializing in commercial properties, especially hotels and restaurants.

Carpenter, Colbert Wood Works, 1992-1996
- Assisted owner of small woodworking shop with all phases of business. Construction of special-order furniture.

TRAINING

1990-1992
On-the-job training at Simpson Construction, sponsored and supervised by International Carpenters Union, Local 7

1987-1990
Apprenticeship program, International Carpenters Union, Local 7

Graduate
Blue Springs Vocational High School

References Available

Erica Yee Park

14 Townsend Road
Boston, Massachusetts 02117
Ericapark@xxx.com

Areas of Expertise

General Construction
Institutional
Commercial
Custom-Built Residential

Projects Completed

St. Catherine's School, Boston
Irving's Red Hots, drive-through restaurant, Boston
Roth Laboratories, scientific research and development center, Philadelphia
Sanchez & Company, hair salon, Philadelphia

Work History

1999 to Present
Owner, Yee Park Construction, Inc., Boston

1996 to 1999
Construction Supervisor, Kevin Gray Company, Philadelphia

Personal and Business References Available

DEBRA ALEXANDER, AIA

1102 Hobbs Road
Portland, ME 04101
(207) 555-9877
debraalexander@xxx.com

SKILLS

◆ Contract administration
◆ Inspection of on-site safety conditions
◆ Preparation of construction documents
◆ On-site and in-house supervision
◆ Development of budgets
◆ Site planning
◆ Carpentry

SAMPLE PROJECTS: AUGUST 1999 TO PRESENT

HARBOR POINT SKILLED NURSING CENTER

Conversion of Harbor Point School of Music into a 320-room state-of-the-art medical center. Created successful remodeling plan. Coordinated work of Building Department, lender, legal counsel, and client.

CEDAR RIDGE APARTMENT COMPLEX

Reroofing of entire structure. Creation of all construction documents and specifications. On-site construction supervision to assure quality control and compliance with all building codes and safety regulations.

FREEPORT AFFORDABLE HOUSING PRJECT

Designed and built single-family home prototype for new state-sponsored affordable housing project. Created plans, ordered materials, and supervised construction on-site. Met with City Planning Commission monthly to report progress. Assisted in creation of policies and procedures manual for use in future projects.

PORTLAND CULTURAL ARTS CENTER

Implemented post-bid adjustments to budget to bring expenditures into line with grant-based budget. Initiated cost/benefit analysis and instituted cost-cutting measures through careful space planning and materials selection.

SAMPLE PROJECTS (CONT.)

SILVER LAKE WILDERNESS CENTER

Upgraded all exterior details. Extensive waterproofing, drainage, and roofing improvement. Coordination of roofing, structural engineering, and design consultants. Preparation of construction drawings for review by Department of Wilderness Preservation.

EDUCATION

University of California, Berkeley, College of Environmental Design, B. Arch., 1998

University of Maine, continuing education courses, computer science and business management, ongoing

MEMBERSHIPS

American Institute of Architects
Women in Architecture

LICENSE

State of Maine #R9383

References will be provided upon request.

Chapter 6

Sample Cover Letters

This chapter contains many sample cover letters for people pursuing a wide variety of jobs and careers in high-tech fields, or who have had experience in these fields in the past.

There are many different styles of cover letters in terms of layout, level of formality, and presentation of information. These samples also represent people with varying amounts of education and work experience. Choose one cover letter or borrow elements from several different cover letters to help you construct your own.

JOHN HOPEWELL

642 BRADY ROAD • WESTFIELD, NJ 07901
201-555-4900 • CELL: 201-555-7556
JOHNHOPEWELL@XXX.COM

October 4, 20--

P.O. Box 687
Trenton, NJ 08607

Dear Colleagues,

The enclosed resume explains in detail my qualifications for the architectural opening you recently advertised in *Architectural News*.

My background includes excellent academic credentials and more than 10 years' experience in all stages of architectural design and construction. I am a generalist whose work has included both commercial and residential properties.

In addition to the specific abilities and job experience listed on my resume, I have a strong aesthetic sense, effective communication skills, and a high degree of devotion to my work. Please find a portfolio of my work online at johnhopewell.com.

You may phone me at 201-555-4900 or write to me at the above address if you wish to arrange an interview.

Sincerely,

John Hopewell

Peter Ainsworth
34 Burling Street
Northbrook, IL 60062
847-555-4857
peterainsworth@xxx.com

May 24, 20--

Ms. Barbara Mendez
Garden Gate Inc.
87 Dundee Road
Elmhurst, IL 60126

Dear Ms. Mendez:

Hope Barlow suggested that I write to inquire about possible job openings at Garden Gate. I recently assisted Ms. Barlow with the walled English garden project at South Shore Botanical Gardens. My work there was part of my senior project for completion of my B.S. in landscape design from Hartsville College.

The enclosed resume explains the English garden project in more detail, describes my experience at Fredrick's Nursery, and summarizes my relevant course work at Hartsville.

After graduation I hope to find an entry-level position as a landscape designer. I would appreciate hearing of any such openings at Garden Gate, and I look forward to the possibility of working with you in the future.

Sincerely,

Peter Ainsworth

Suzanne Parker

8411 Ainsie Blvd.
Boulder, CO 80304
303-555-6948
suzanneparker@xxx.com

March 11, 20--

Karen Schiff
Senior Design Consultant
Schiff Interiors
76 Dell Place, Ste. 402
Denver, CO 80209

Dear Ms. Schiff:

Your recent lecture, "Interior Landscaping: Bringing the Outdoors In," was the highlight of Design Expo 2003. The atriums, greenhouses, and rooftop gardens your firm designs transform urban spaces, bringing the beauty and tranquility usually associated with more pastoral settings to the city.

Your incorporation of these "green spaces" into your designs has inspired me to offer my services as a subcontractor/consultant. You indicated at the conference that your firm is quite busy at the moment—an enviable but hectic situation for you! I specialize in landscape design, and my clients include architects, urban planners, and interior designers. Many of my clients subcontract a portion of the design to me. My recent projects have ranged from consulting work for a mall developer to designing a large flower garden for a local estate owner planning her daughter's wedding.

I am enclosing my resume as well as a description of my business that appeared last year in an article in *Country Gardens*.

I look forward to working with you.

Cordially,

Suzanne Parker

Zamir Achibee
65 Lakeview Road
Palo Alto, CA 94304

August 3, 20--

Lawrence Hartman
4590 King Drive
Palo Alto, CA 94304

Dear Mr. Hartman:

I have long admired the design of the Harrington Retirement Center, where my father resides. So it was with great interest that I learned, via your ad in last Sunday's *Palo Alto Gazette*, of your current opening for a senior architect. I hope that after you review my enclosed resume, you will agree that my skills and experience match your firm's current needs.

As my resume indicates, I have been self-employed for the past five years. Running my own architectural business has been satisfying and profitable, but I do miss the interaction with colleagues that an in-house position provides.

I will be out of town on business from August 10 to 15. After that, I am available at your convenience if you wish to arrange an interview. I am most easily reached by phone in the early morning at 818-555-1324 or by E-mail at zamirachibee@xxx.com.

Thanks for your consideration of my credentials.

Yours truly,

Zamir Achibee

Warren J. Kilpatrick
Rockwell Associates
1302 Wright Lane
Culverton, VA 12245

June 3, 20--

Kirsten Sullivan
Arabesque, Inc.
604 W. Brentwood Road
Culverton, VA 12245

Dear Ms. Sullivan:

Thank you for calling Rockwell Associates this morning regarding the possible redesign of your property on Riley Road for use as a dance studio. As you suggested, I should tour the property with you in the near future to determine how the space could best be reconfigured to meet the needs of your new business. But first, let me provide you with more information about Rockwell Associates and my own credentials as an architect.

I've worked for Rockwell for the past five years. You may be familiar with our projects, which have included the new city hall and the restoration of the Barclay Theater. For two years prior to my association with Rockwell, I was an independent contractor specializing in residential rehabilitation. My resume, which explains my career in more detail, is enclosed. I would also be pleased to furnish a list of references should you want them.

I feel confident that together we could meet the challenge of converting the Riley Road property into a unique space for your new business, and I look forward to meeting with you to discuss the design options. Please call me at 703-555-9804, ext. 32, or E-mail me at warrenkilpatrick@xxx.com, to arrange an appointment.

Sincerely,

Warren J. Kilpatrick

Carlotta Hernandez

652 Menard Lane
Boulder, Colorado 80301
(303) 555-5958
carlottahernandez@xxx.com

Steven Clarke
King Design and Construction
23 Madison Street
Denver, CO 80209

July 9, 20--

Dear Mr. Clarke:

Is your firm in need of a hardworking, experienced architectural drafter?
I can offer your organization the following skills:

- Ability to develop creative, cost-effective construction plans for residential and commercial building projects
- Experience with AutoCAD and DesignCAD computer programs
- Hands-on construction background that enhances my troubleshooting skills
- Complete, current knowledge of fire and safety regulations and building codes
- Strong work ethic and close attention to detail
- Proven ability to meet deadlines

It would be my pleasure to work with your firm. I will call you before the end of the month to discuss possible job openings. Should you wish to contact me in the meantime, please feel free to call me at the number below.

Thank you for your time and consideration.

Sincerely,

Carlotta Hernandez

REGINALD SMITH

1402 Winchester, No. 106 • Chicago, IL 60645
(312) 555-8611 • reginaldsmith@xxx.com

August 14, 20--

Northwestern Bank
4260 Harlem Avenue
Chicago, IL 60641

ATTN:
Mrs. Carlotta Jimenez
Human Resources Director

I was pleased to see your recent notice in the *Chicago Tribune* for a construction coordinator. My experience managing the daily aspects of construction sites closely matches your requirements.

My recent job history is as follows:

Owner, Smith Construction Inc.
Extensive experience in managing all aspects of construction, including estimating, negotiating contracts, scheduling, and supervising job sites.

Superintendent, Warner Construction
Supervisor for commercial remodeling and construction projects, including the Lincoln Towers office complex, Oak Park Medical Building, and Household Bank.

Superintendent, David Wright and Associates
Work included (1) construction of a new prototype warehouse for Stevenson Manufacturing and (2) total remodeling of Commercial Bank. Coordinated work of owners, corporate officers, building manager, tenants, architects, subcontractors, engineers, and city planning department.

As you can see, Mrs. Jimenez, I am a seasoned professional. I believe my diverse experiences over the last fifteen years would enable me to excel as the new construction coordinator for your bank.

I appreciate your consideration.

Sincerely,

Reginald Smith

Lee Herada

Buffalo, New York 14225
418 Range Road

leeherada@xxx.com
212-555-9867
212-555-7766 (Cell)

December 10, 20--

Mr. Charles Berman
426 Second Avenue, Ste. 602
Harrison, NY 10573

Dear Chuck:

Thanks for taking so much time with me on the phone last week. I appreciate having your insight into the perils and possibilities of self-employment. Launching Berman and Brad has certainly been an excellent career move for you, and your dedication to building the firm is impressive. After speaking with you, I am more determined than ever to follow your lead and begin my own career as an independent contractor next year.

As you know, I've worked for Emerson, Inc., since 1998 and have had a wide array of responsibilities:

- Survey & studies of land development projects
- Site selection, facilities planning, and floor layout
- Preparation of models, written proposals, and price quotes for clients
- Participation in financial discussions and contract negotiations with architects, attorneys, bankers, investors, and contractors

Please feel free to share this summary of my credentials, and the enclosed resumes, with your colleagues at Berman and Brad. After the first of the year, I would be pleased to take on any assignments you feel comfortable delegating to me. I would also appreciate hearing of any projects or clients that, for one reason or another, are not of interest to your firm.

You can reach me here at Herada Construction, 212-555-9867, until the 20th, when I am going home to Wisconsin to celebrate Christmas with my family. I will be checking my E-mail during that time also: leeherada@xxx.com.

I hope to have the chance to speak to you again soon. I always enjoy our discussions and feel fortunate to have you as my unofficial mentor.

Best wishes for a safe and happy holiday.

Yours truly,

Lee Herada

Erica Martin, AIA

3123 Glenwood Road • Boston, MA 01936
(617) 555-4206 • ericamartin@xxx.com

July 10, 20--

Mr. Douglas Yee
Yee/Collins Associates
14 S. Washington Street, Suite 401
Boston, MA 01931

Dear Mr. Yee:

Enclosed are the price quotes and blueprints you requested for the addition at Jackson Junior High School. I am confident that you will agree that my design offers a cost-effective way to provide the extra space the school needs. The details of the design address your concerns:

• Dividers allow for yearly variations in class size.
• Floor to ceiling cabinets and built-in bookcases provide teachers with ample storage space.
• Gym is 10 percent larger than existing gyms so that the new gym may be used as a multipurpose room.
• Track lighting at the south end of the new gym is designed for use with existing mobile riser unit during school plays and recitals.

I have also included a copy of my resume for your review. Please note my recent design of the Hilderbrande School of Music. You may wish to visit that building or speak to the school's director, Sarah Weintraub, regarding my work there.

Thanks for giving me the opportunity to bid on this project. I will call late next week to discuss your first impressions of the enclosed design and proposed budget.

Yours truly,

Erica Martin, AIA
Woodside Architectural Group

Linda Carsten

221 Chandler Road
Neavitt, MD 21652
410-555-9532
lindacarsten@xxx.com

October 20, 20--

Peter Long, Manager
Serendipity Architectural Salvage
1602 Hicks Road
Glen Burnie, MD 21062

Dear Mr. Long:

For interior designers, architects, and builders, your shop is a gold mine. I have always enjoyed shopping at Serendipity and recently purchased an antique mantel from you. It was the focal point of my senior design project.

So I was especially pleased to see your ad for an assistant manager in last Sunday's *Gazette*. My background in interior design and my familiarity with your place of business make me an ideal candidate for the position.

I will receive my degree in interior design from the University of Maryland next spring. In the meantime, I am available part-time during the evening and weekend hours you require.

As the enclosed resume indicates, I have previous sales experience. I worked for two summers at Memory Lane Antiques. My supervisor there was owner Karen Stafford. She is willing to provide a reference, and you may contact her at 410-555-4095 or by E-mail at karenstafford@xxx.com.

In addition to meeting the stated requirements for the position of assistant manager, I can offer your customers the benefit of my growing knowledge of interior design. I can explain the age, history, and composition of the pieces you sell and suggest creative uses for them.

Please consider me for the position of assistant manager. I would enjoy providing your customers with the same excellent service I have always received at Serendipity.

Sincerely,

Linda Carsten

October 3, 20--

Mr. James Hansen
James Hansen Galleries
442 Kingston Circle
New York, NY 10014

Dear Mr. Hansen:

I recently visited Hansen Galleries for the opening of the Sven Jacobs Exhibition, where I met your assistant, Lee Winters. She mentioned that you are considering converting a loft space on Winston Road for use as a second gallery. This news is of great interest to me because I specialize in the design of art galleries, studios, and performance spaces here in New York.

The enclosed resume will provide you with the details of my education and professional experience. My philosophy of design is more difficult to summarize, but I can briefly explain my usual approach.

I tend to work with the existing elements as much as possible rather than imposing a predetermined style or layout on an existing space. With older buildings, preservation of the original construction materials is always my goal. Removing, restoring, and reinstalling original fixtures is my standard way of working. I seek out vintage fixtures and materials if restoration of the existing ones is not feasible. My designs tend toward subtle changes and traditional approaches rather than radical reconstruction or trendy architectural details.

Because I design for artists who tend to have a finely tuned aesthetic sense, I seek as much input from clients as possible during the initial phases of any project. At the same time, I feel comfortable letting clients know when specific requests are out of sync with the overall design or are architecturally unsound. Each finished project is always the result of careful collaboration with the client.

Perhaps we may be able to collaborate on the creation of your second gallery. I will call early next week to discuss your plans.

Cordially,

Alexis Palmer
602 W. Hanley Road
New York, NY 10233
212-555-8877
alexispalmer@xxx.com

RICHARD HOPKINS

212 Broad Street
Houston, Texas 94117
713-555-8765
richardhopkins@xxx.com

November 4, 20--

Ms. Anita Drakulic, Director
Office of Urban Development
411 Wallace Street
Houston, TX 77292

Dear Ms. Drakulic:

I submit the enclosed resume in response to your announced search for a new director for the Zoning and Permits Department. Currently I own my own consulting firm, which assists corporations and entrepreneurs in conducting marketing studies, designing business proposals, and relocating manufacturing operations worldwide. Although I enjoy the challenge of owning my own business, I am always seeking new opportunities to expand my experience and to serve the community.

As you will note after reviewing my resume, my professional experience is diverse. The common thread is a core of basic skills I'm sure you value:

• Community relations
• Communications
• Fund-raising
• Marketing
• Cost accounting
• Labor mediation
• Contract negotiations

Thank you for taking time to consider my qualifications. I am available at your convenience if you wish to schedule an interview.

Sincerely,

Richard Hopkins

Mr. Kevin Goldberg, AIA
185 Edens Lane
Fort Lauderdale, FL 33340
(305) 555-8986
kevingoldberg@xxx.com

March 11, 20--

Mark Robert Schneider, AIA
Rinehart & Schneider, Inc.
101 DeWitt Road
Fort Lauderdale, FL 33340

Dear Mr. Schneider:

I enjoyed our conversation Monday evening following the City Council meeting. As you go forward with site studies and planning for the new civic center, please be aware of my willingness to serve as a consultant.

Last fall I retired from Ashberry and Royalton, where I served as senior architect for fifteen years. In addition to a lengthy career in architecture, I have worked as an engineering design consultant. My experience has been diverse, and I am well versed in all stages of client relations, project management, planning, and design. Therefore, I would feel comfortable providing advice at this early planning stage on issues such as contract negotiations, block layouts, stacking plans, test layouts, or space planning. Perhaps later in the process, you might also need assistance with engineering coordination or field observation. The enclosed resume details my experience in these areas and describes project highlights from my engineering and architectural careers.

Rinehart & Schneider enjoys an enviable reputation throughout the state and beyond. City officials have chosen well in selecting your firm for the development and construction of the civic center. Please let me know if I may assist you with any aspect of this exciting new venture.

Best wishes,

Kevin Goldberg, AIA

Lisa Holmes

4226 Gleason Road • Skokie, IL 60646
847-555-7986 (work) • 847-555-8997 (home)
lisaholmes@xxx.com

January 10, 20--

Chicago Architecture Foundation
345 LaSalle Street
Chicago, IL 60604

ATTN: Personnel Department

Ladies and Gentlemen:

Few cities have the rich architectural heritage that Chicago enjoys. As a lifelong Chicago resident, I have always appreciated the city's architectural diversity and sophistication. The possibility of sharing my enthusiasm with others appeals to me. That's why I am submitting the enclosed resume in response to your ad for an educational director.

My current title is Director of Educational Development Programs at the Skokie Public Library. The position offers me the challenge of designing a wide variety of community outreach programs including literacy tutoring, computer education courses, special interest seminars, and boards to design educational enrichment programs for all district students, from the elementary to the secondary level. These programs have included summer reading, story hours, and homework assistance.

In addition to planning and implementing educational programs, I am an experienced fund-raiser. I have helped fund educational projects at the library through successful grant writing and organization of the annual Historic Home Tour.

The skills I have developed at the library would transfer well to the position of educational director at the Chicago Architecture Foundation. I would be glad to meet at your convenience to discuss my skills and your current educational goals. You may reach me at 847-555-7986 between 9 and 5, in the evenings at 847-555-8997, or by E-mail at lisaholmes@xxx.com. I look forward to hearing from you.

Sincerely,

Lisa Holmes

Barbara Remington

Remington Home Inspection, Inc.,
322 Harrison Street • St. Louis, MO 63146
800-555-9866 • barbararemington@xxx.com

February 11, 20--

ATTN:
Kathleen Borowski
Quality Realty
2106 Keen Road
St. Louis, MO 63146

A new home. It's still part of the American Dream. But statistics show that today's "new" home is usually previously owned. The beautiful façade of an older home may hide costly problems. That's why so many savvy home buyers invest in the superior home inspection services my company offers.

Why is our service so popular? Because we offer knowledge, service, and guarantees you won't get from our competitors. Most inspectors base their reports on a visual inspection and offer no warranty. Our service is different.

The Once-Over
Our initial inspection includes all appliances, electrical outlets, walls, ceilings, flooring, foundations, roofing, heating and cooling systems, sewage system, water and electrical supplies, and exterior cement work.

The Troubleshooters
Whenever our inspectors detect a problem, they undertake a second, more invasive inspection, accompanied by an in-house specialist. Our staff includes professional plumbers and electricians and a structural engineer.

Guaranteed Peace of Mind
At Remington Home Inspection, we stand behind our work. We offer each client a written one-year warranty.

Buying a new home can be a stressful experience. It's a big decision. I hope you will take a moment to review my enclosed resume and consider the peace of mind my company can offer your clients. It might be the finishing touch that helps you make your next sale!

Barbara Remington
President

Enclosures: Resume
Price List
Sample Inspection Report

Michael Lee
137 Cindy Ct.
Burleson, Texas 76103
(817) 555-8986
m.lee@xxx.com

August 12, 20--

Dear Sir or Madam,

Please find enclosed my resume. I think you'll agree that my experience as an Architectural/Engineering Consultant qualifies me for the position you have posted for a Project Manager. I have acted as the Project Manager on several local construction sites and ensured that each met deadlines and budgetary requirements. I am a skilled personnel manager, and my years of experience allow me to anticipate challenges and meet them with proven methods.

I am available for a personal interview at your earliest convenience. I will call your office next Wednesday to ensure you received this resume and, hopefully, schedule a meeting. I look forward to speaking with you then.

Sincerely,

Michael Lee

Joanne Williams
135 Washington St.
Boston, MA 02111
617-555-3824
joannewilliams@xxx.com

August 12, 20--

Dear Sir or Madam,

I recently saw your ad for an assistant interior decorator and would like
to present my skills for your review. I am currently enrolled at the University of Maryland, studying interior design, and have excelled in my
course work. Several of my projects have received awards in student
design competitions, and I would like to bring my talent and imagination
to your firm.

Your designs are well known throughout the industry, and I am eager to
add to your reputation as a design house with innovative, fresh ideas and
a dedication to style.

Please find my resume and references enclosed. I will be graduating this
spring and am eager to start my career. I hope to hear from you soon to
schedule an interview so I can show you my portfolio filled with award-
winning designs.

Sincerely,

Joanne Williams

Casey Corbett, AIA

8162 Alden Road
Morrisville, VT 05661
802-555-4553
caseycorbett@xxx.com

August 12, 20--

Dear Sir,

With nearly a decade of experience throughout the construction industry, I'm not only fully qualified for whatever role you need filled, I'm excited to bring that experience to a new challenge. I am a fully licensed architect and a certified land surveyor, which allows me to draft innovative plans with practical expectations. I not only understand the need for creative design, I also understand the importance of feasibility and economy.

I have an extensive portfolio with projects ranging in size and budget. I can provide those and a list of references at your request, and I hope to be able to prove to you my value as an employee.

Please feel free to contact me at any time. I look forward to your call.

Sincerely,

Casey Corbett

Patrick O'Connor
1325 Beaubine Ct.
Buffalo, New York 14225
212-555-9867
212-555-7766 (Cell)
poconnor@xxx.com

August 13, 20--

Dear Sir or Madam,

I am a skilled and capable contractor with nearly ten years' experience in the construction field. Having been a construction company owner myself, I can identify the needs of your company and maintain a profitable work site while managing crews and materials. My experience as a Project Manager uniquely qualifies me to not only coordinate subcontractors but also to assist in site surveys and material selection. I think you'll agree that my experience would be an asset to your organization, and I hope to meet with you soon to discuss your opportunities.

I am available for personal interviews anytime in the next two weeks. I will then be out of town for ten days on a previously arranged engagement. Please feel free to contact me at your convenience.

Sincerely,

Patrick O'Connor